A JOURNEY

FROM

ORENBURG TO BOKHARA

IN THE YEAR 1820.

EDITED BY

BARON VON MEYENDORF,

Colonel on the General Staff of His Majesty the Emperor of Russia, and revised by the Chevalier Amadée Jaubert.

[AFTER THE FRENCH ORIGINAL COMPILED BY Dr. CARL HERMANN SCHEIDLER,
ESPECIALLY PRINTED WITH THE ETHNOGRAPHICAL ARCHIVES.]

JENA 1826.

TRANSLATED BY

CAPTAIN E. F. CHAPMAN, R.H.A.

CALCUTTA:

PRINTED AT THE FOREIGN DEPARTMENT PRESS,
COUNCIL HOUSE STREET.
1870.

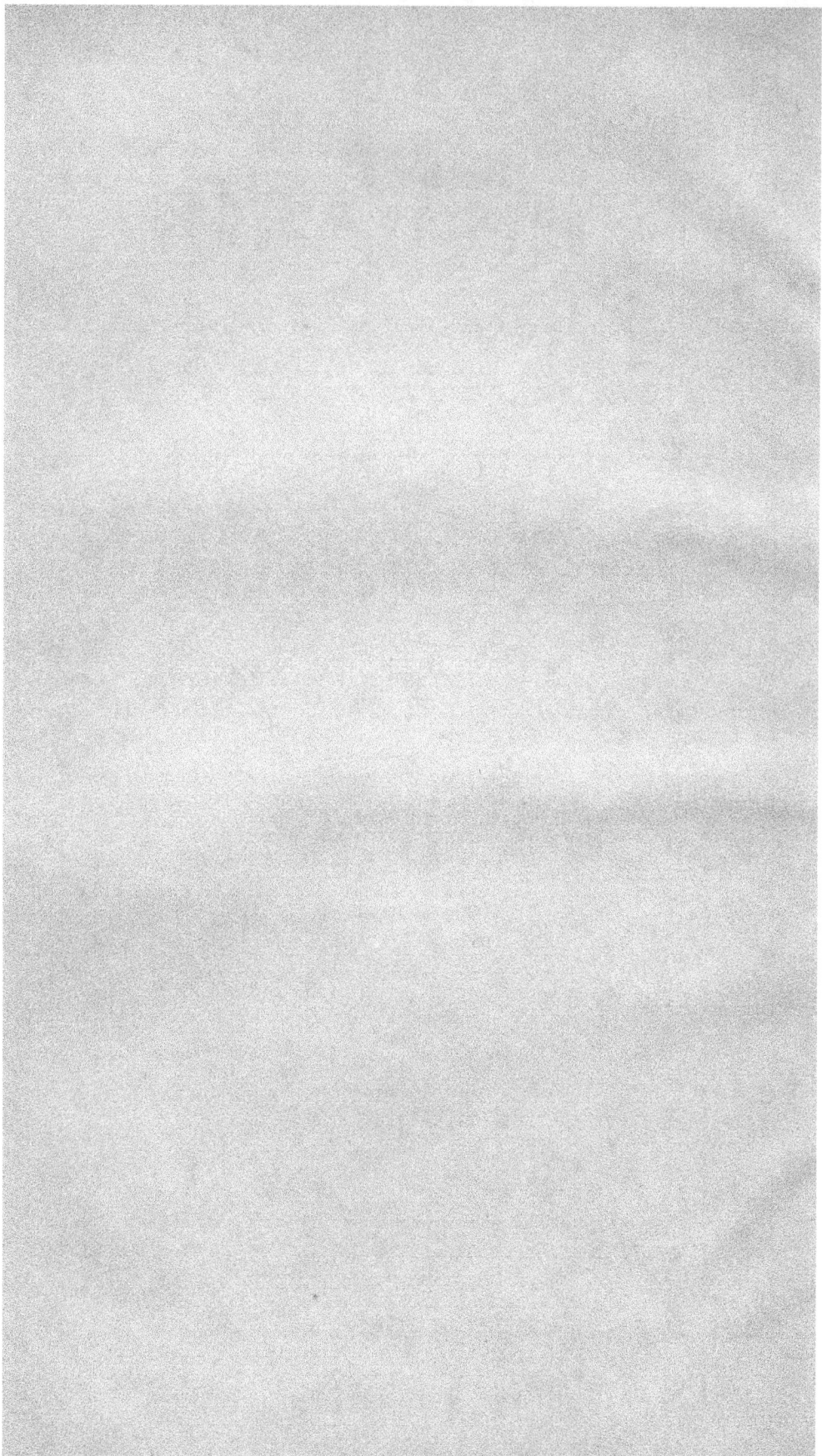

PREFACE.

THE Author has written the following description of one of the least known countries and people of Asia in the French language, to further its general advertisement as well as to secure its being more carefully printed in Paris and to allow of its perusal by the well-known Orientalist Jaubert, because an important number of Turkish, Mongolian, and Persian names are mentioned. The complete title of the work is as follows :—

"Voyage d'Orenburg à Boukhara, fait en 1820, à travers les steppes qur s'etendent à l'est de la mer Oral et au delà de l'encien Jaxartes: redigé par M. le Baron Georges de Meyendorf Colonel à l'état—major de S. M. l'Empereur de toutes les Russies; et revu par M. le Chevalier Amedée Jaubert; Maitre des réquètes honoraire, Professeur de Turc à l'ecole Royale et spéciale établie près la Bibliotheque du Roi, l'un des Secrétaires Interprètes de S. M. pour les langues orientales, &c., Paris. Libraire Orientale de Dondey Duprèe, 1826."

Beyond the occasion and the preparation for the voyage, the Author treats, in his introduction, of the following :— The commercial relations between Russia and Bokhara had received very great extension since the last half of the 18th century, and Bokharian Envoys frequently journeyed to St. Petersburgh: one of these, who came to that capital in the years 1816 and 1820, expressed, on the part of the Khan of Bokhara, the wish of this last that a Russian Embassy might be accredited to Bokhara.

The Emperor Alexander gave attention to this, and was inclined towards it; for he thought the result of this proposal would not only afford extension to the commercial relations which already existed between the States, but that it would also tend to develop regions of fresh knowledge, of which, especially till now, very little was ascertained: for which reason the Emperor nominated as his representative with the Khan of Bokhara, Herr Councillor and Secretary of Legation Von Negri; of the College Senate, Von Jacoolew; and Dr. Pander, a remarkably cultivated German Naturalist; and three interpreters from Orenburg were attached to the expedition. Baron Von Meyendorf undertook the charge of compiling the Geographical and Statistical records of the countries through which they would pass, and had, to assist him in this work, Herrn Volkonsky and Semosryf, Lieutenants on the Staff. In June 1820 the authorized members of this Embassy received orders to hold themselves in readiness for the journey, and in August they had reached Orenburg, distant 2,200 versts from St. Petersburgh.

As the way lay shut in between the immeasurable steppes through which it stretched, in which only plundering hordes rove about, the Russian Government gave the Embassy 2 Field-pieces and an escort amounting to 200 Cossacks, 200 Infantry soldiers, and 25 mounted followers: 358 camels carried the baggage, and the number of led horses amounted to 400. With respect to the history of the journey, the Author claims attention to the fact that the incompleteness of his account is due, in part, to the ignorance which prevails in Bokhara itself, the population of which does not concern itself with affairs that have no relation either to their religion or their trade, partly to the excessive distrust which this people, in common with all Orientals, exhibit to an unlimited extent, especially in their relations with Europeans, and which the Khan ordered his followers to observe in all intimate dealings with the Russians. Beyond this he feels able to assure us that what is here communicated is ascertained with certainty, and is reliable; it possesses the advantage of novelty, since it treats of a country so little visited.

A JOURNEY

FROM

ORENBURG TO BOKHARA

IN THE

YEAR 1820.

⸺◦:◦:◦⸺

CHAPTER I.

Preparations for the Journey. Departure from Orenburg. The Route.

The persons appointed to the Embassy to Bokhara reached Orenburg in the course of August 1820; the Cossacks and Baschkirees alone, whom the General-in-Chief, Von Essen, had nominated and appointed to be our escort, could not be ready to march till the middle of September, and so, meanwhile, consequent on the multiplicity of preparations, we saw the beautiful season of the year pass away. On economical grounds we had wished, in the first instance, to load the necessary provisions in waggons, but the particular enquiry which we made into the nature of the country through which we had to travel induced us to select camels chiefly for that purpose, and only to take 25 waggons for those who might be sick upon the road or might otherwise come to grief: each of these waggons was yoked with three horses and was driven by a Baschkiree. As we had to cross several streams in the Kirghiz Steppes two vessels or "bateaux" were sent with us, that were loaded in carts; these were so constructed that by uniting the boats a raft could be formed capable of bearing about 20 men.

A march of two months in the desert required for each soldier 105lbs. of biscuit and for every horse four centners of oats; further, a measured quantity of oatmeal; a double supply of ammunition for our two field-pieces, a dozen kibitkas or tents of felt, 200 kegs for the transport of water in the desert, and, lastly, other casks of spirit: 320 camels were laden with provisions for the escort, and 38 with baggage and supplies for the servants of the Embassy.

The Military Governor had made a compact with the Chief of the Kirghizzees, by power of which he would receive 110 paper-rubles (about 110 francs as a paper-ruble and a franc are of about equal money value,) if he brought the 380 camels which we required to Orenburg by the 15th September, but before this anxiously expected day not a single Kirghizzee could be seen.

The market at Orenburg was not furnished with the quantity of oats demanded for our escort, and we were forced to allow the dealers to arrange for its purchase from neighbouring estates (that is to say, a distance of 150 versts).

The cost of the entertainment of the escort during their absence from Russia was calculated at about 72,000 rubles, which we were obliged to have stored up in hand in order to provide them with the necessary provisions in Bokhara. As the export of Russian money is, however, forbidden, we were obliged to purchase ducats; the merchants of Orenburg had, however, no very large quantity in hand, and as they had visited in vain the distant town of Tronk, 600 versts from Orenburg, in order to effect the exchange, we were forced to despatch a courier 1,500 versts to Moscow, who obtained the required sum from the Bank there.

Thus several unforeseen hindrances postponed our departure more and more; the favourable season had already passed, the half of September elapsed, and already sharp frosts set in; the bad season commenced, rain, hail, and snow came in turns each day, and thus I saw myself about to undertake a journey during the heavy rain storms and frosts of the months of October and November.

I recalled the despondency and sufferings of Timur on the Sihun which Cherefeddin depicts. "Some," says he, "lost noses and ears, others saw their feet and hands drop off from their bodies; the sky was nothing but a single cloud, and the earth a solitary snow flake." The points which we had to cross were, besides, further to the north than those at which the army of the celebrated Robber perished, and I pitied our poor soldiers, who, without furs, were to encounter the perils of a winter which was there always very severe.

We held several conferences with the Kirghizzees in order to learn something of the road we had to pursue, and to discover, beforehand, the difficulties which it placed before us.

Five of them were chosen as our guides, and the most respectable nominated as their principal, as well as, at the same time, some 60 more selected for watching, leading, and loading the camels. These last-named animals are accustomed to be distributed in "Kochs," or droves of from 20 to 60 head, which are conducted each by a petty Kirghiz Chief, and the loading is also distributed amongst particular "Kochs."

9th October.—The last camel which was required by us arrived, and our departure was definitively settled for the following morning.

10th October.—The assembled escort was reviewed by the Governor-General in the market-place of Orenburg. He alluded to the importance of the service and blessed the travellers. The religious enthusiasm, the sacred reserve, the "blessing" which precede so wearisome a travel through immeasurable wastes!—all these make a deep and solemn impression, the importance of which is strengthened both by the anticipation of the unknown accidents of fortune, and the risks which such an undertaking can suggest.

The dangers, indeed, ranged themselves in a formidable group. It was possible that the Kirghizzees, always anxious for plunder, and always objecting to see the Russians traverse their wastes, might harass us with night attacks, an apprehension which seems to be warranted, since in 1803, not far from the Sir Daria, Lieutenant Gaverdovsky was attacked by the Kirghizzees, and only succeeded in saving his life by the most determined resistance; but his wife, his physician, and three-fourths of his escort fell into the power of the nomads of the desert. If, however, they should not dare to attack so strong an escort as ours, they could burn all the grass and reeds over which our road passed, so as to render more serious the difficulties of the journey, or perhaps to make it quite impossible of accomplishment.

Another very common method of attack with them is to slink in, during the night, amongst the horses at graze and hurry off a large number with inconceivable rapidity, a contingency which was so much the more to be feared as it was altogether impossible to repair the injury it might inflict. General Von Essen, who foresaw these dangers, gladly accepted the offer which the Kirghiz Sultan, Harun Ghazl, Abul Ghazl, made him, to accompany the Embassy as far as the Sir, with several hundred Kirghizzees whose faith he could rely upon. The General placed the more value on this offer that it must have a vast moral influence upon the entire race of the Khirghizzees.

However, the inhabitants of Khiva who occupy the countries to the south of the Sea of Aral seem more to be feared than even the Kirghizzees, since each plundering band does not wander about in a weak condition, but they are more united, and frequently undertake robbing expeditions with a strength of 4,000 or 5,000 men; although such a mass of horsemen could scarcely intimidate our infantry, yet our escort would, in addition to making a suitable resistance, be called upon to protect a convoy of 700 camels (having regard to those which, in consequence of the protection we afforded, the Bokharian merchants were sending with us); added to which the robber hordes, during their sudden and unexpected attacks upon the caravans, are in the habit of using the truly warlike stratagem of frightening the camels by wild cries, which, when once they are thrown into confusion, easily become their prey.

The best means to meet this is to make these animals lie down at once, when they can only be persuaded to raise themselves again with infinite trouble. Only, often one has no time for the adoption of this precautionary measure, and then the caravan is lost: then how easy is it to conceive that, without camels, a sojourn in the Kirghiz waste is the greatest of dangers, for one must often pay for such a want with one's life.

Beyond the dangers of the road, we might touch upon those to be encountered in Bokhara itself, a country governed by a warlike and wild race. In fact, Bokharian merchants, before the journey commenced, assured their friends that probably none of the Christians would return to their own country, even though the Khan of Khiva allowed them to pass; but that the Khan would scarcely be guilty of the fault of permitting those who had spied out his country to come back.

Under such auspices were we forced to commence our journey, the route of which is here communicated as a key to this fragment.

Route traversed by the Russian Embassy from Orenburg to Bokhara.

Date.	Camp.	What was found.	Versts.	Toises.
10 October	Stream Berdianka	Water and pasturage	20	251
12 ,,	,, Bitli-su	Little water	25	469
13 ,,	,, Burteh	Water	33	280
14 ,,	Onzim-Burteh	Water, pasturage, and shrubs	26	126
16 ,,	Cara-Batak	Woods, shrubs, water, and pasturage	35	302
17 ,,	River Ilek	,, ,, ,, ,,	27	434
19 ,,	,, ,,	,, ,, ,, ,,	31	60
20 ,,	Stream Tamby-i-aman	,, ,, ,, ,,	27	580
21 ,,	,, Suruk-sir	Shrubs, reeds, water, pasturage	29	470
23 ,,	,, Talach-beg	,, water, pasturage	35	37
24 ,,	Hill of Bassaghi	No water, little pasturage and shrubs	31	386
25 ,,	River Kubleili-temir	Shrubs, little pasturage, water saline	28	89
27 ,,	,, Tiraklu	Good water, little pasturage and shrubs	31	219
28 ,,	Stream Cara-a-Kenti	Bad water, little pasturage and shrubs	34	210
30 ,,	,, Tuban	Water, shrubs, pasturage	27	123
31 ,,	,, Kaoundjar	,, ,, ,,	22	101
1 Nov.	,, ,,	,, ,, ,,	29	210
2 ,,	Lake Kobia	Water, reeds, pasturage	41	454
4 ,,	Springs Cul Kuduk	The same with shrubs	29	329
6 ,,	Adji-Kubuk	,, ,, ,,	24	385
7 ,,	Tchuber Tepit	Saline water, reeds, pasturage, and shrubs	29	35
8 ,,	Wells of Ok-tani	Bad water, shrubs, and pasturage	26	432
9 ,,	,, of Cari-Butak	,, pasturage and few shrubs	39	292
11 ,,	Hills of Devman-bachi	No water, shrubs, pasturage	30	161
12 ,,	Springs of Uratschai	Bad water and pasturage, shrubs	26	162
13 ,,	Kulli	,, pasturage, saline water, shrubs	30	268
14 ,,	Hills of Sapak	No pasturage, no water, shrubs	26	162
15 ,,	Baz of Camechlu-bagh	Good water, little pasturage and shrubs	25	219
18 ,,	Jalter-Kul	,, good pasturage, few shrubs	27	19
19 ,,	River Sir Daria	Reeds, water, pasturage	9	378
22 ,,	Little lake without name	,, ,, ,,	24	79
24 ,,	River Kuban	Few shrubs, rushes, good water	19	504
25 ,,	,, ,,	,, ,, ,,	16	249
27 ,,	,, ,,	,, ,, ,,	28	14
30 ,,	Place without name	Shrubs, little pasture, no water	30	40
1 Dec.	D'jan-Daria	,, ,, bad water	33	449
3 ,,	Near the sands of Kizil-Kum	,, neither pasture nor water	36	109
4 ,,	Sand plain of Kizil-Kum	,, ,, ,,	42	162
5 ,,	,, ,,	,, ,, ,,	44	69
6 ,,	Near the same	,, no water, little pasture	46	5
7 ,,	Springs, Yorz-Kuduk	Good water, little pasture, and shrubs	43	311
9 ,,	Spot without a name	No water	43	300
10 ,,	Near the land of Balak	,, shrubs, little pasture	43	182
11 ,,	Hills Gusiq-Cara	,, ,, ,,	38	442
12 ,,	Wells Cara Aghatscha	Few shrubs, saline water, no pasture	40	38
13 ,,	,, Aghatina	,, ,, ,,	38	275
15 ,,	Springs, Odum-Kuduk	Good water, few shrubs, no pasture	38	386
16 ,,	Village Kaghatan	⎫	17	366
17 ,,	Town of Waskend	⎬ Cultivated country	17	289
18 ,,	Village Basarschi	⎭	23	169
20 ,,	Bokhara		2	......

CHAPTER II.

A Kirghiz-Aoul. Sultan Harun Ghazl. Ilek-Kubleili-temir.

We shall divide the entire road traversed by the expedition into three parts, the first of which comprises the whole space from Orenburg to the hills of Murghodjar, which we passed between the streams of Cara-a-Kenti and Tuban; the second, the territory between those hills and the Sir Daria; and the third, that lying between that river and Bokhara.

The character of the land of the first-named tract is uniform throughout; one observes an undulating country cut up by rows of hills, and in consequence of the scarcity of wood and the lowness of the elevation, one has an unvarying horizon, in which the eye seeks in vain an object on which to repose.

Arid uniformity and silence characterize the steppe. Throughout its entire extent of four hundred and thirty-four miles, one discovers trees in two places only; moreover, everywhere only small prickly shrubs sprouting three feet in height, and but sparingly distributed, so that the eye of an European is unable to support the monotony of this horrible desert.

We crossed a tolerably large number of streams, all of which had a similar appearance and ran in the same direction. From the Aral to the Sir they are all fordable, and are dried up in the summer and autumn. Moreover, the Ilek, the Emba, the Temir, or Tighiz, have the name of rivers, and usually possess water, although commonly of slight depth. Several small streams completely dry up in summer, others distribute themselves in a row of small lakes, frequently two yards in depth, only united by small tricklings, thus almost without connection. Every year the steppe is covered by an immense mass of snow, which, at the commencement of spring, is melted by the great heat, and by which the streams rise to a remarkable height and attain a tearing velocity.

Thirty versts from Orenburg, I discovered on the highest of the neighbouring hills, the Djilauhi-tepeh, a belemnite and an ammon's horn; and between the Onzim-Burteh and Cara-Batak, as well as on this side as far as the hills of Murghodjar, I saw these fossils, as well as mussels, in great numbers.

The soil is usually argillaceous, dry, hard, and distributed in several shades of colour. The hills, as a rule, have rounded tops and gradual inclines, as though the force of water had smoothed the unevenness of the ground; near the small hills of Bassaghi we saw several petrifactions, mollusks, and even the tooth of a shark (dog-fish?), all of which appeared to indicate to us the signs of an ancient sea bed. At Berdianka we noticed the traces of exhausted copper mines, which Pallas mentions, and at Kiziloral several others. At about seven versts from our camping ground by the Onzim-Burteh we discovered, by following the stream upwards, coal-pits; we tried the coals in our smithy, and they burnt very well.

At Cara-Batak we were pleasantly sheltered by a group of small alders, and on the banks of the Ilek shrubs and trees exist, to wit, poplars and willows, which, owing to the vicinity of the desert, delight the eye of the traveller. The pasturage near, the river is, moreover, particularly good, so that the Kirghizzees have a special preference for that neighbourhood.

The Ilek is the largest stream which we crossed on this side the Sir; its breadth approaches 10 toises: its velocity over a gravel bed is considerable, and carp, perch, pike and gudgeon, carrasius (carp-like fish), and other sorts of fish are caught in it.

On its bank we observed at one time a large Kirghiz village or "Aoul" of fifty tents of white and brown felt, which were erected in irregular groups of from three to six.

Flocks of sheep which might be reckoned at from 5,000 to 6,000 attracted in the first place our attention. We soon discovered that this encampment belonged to the above-mentioned Sultan Harun Ghazl, the most distinguished head of the Kirghizzees, who was ready to accompany us as far as the Sir, and thus to afford a proof of his leaning towards the Russian Government, whose support he sadly needed in his perpetual feud with the Khan of Khiva. The morning after our arrival the Sultan was on horseback in order to visit Herr Von Negri; he was surrounded by about a hundred Kirghizzees, and wore a turban, a practice which is not customary in these deserts, but is considered, in that place, the sign of a special religious devotion in a Mahomedan Kirghizzee. He had a healthy complexion, large, good-looking eyes, and a pleasant as well as earnest expression: we could easily perceive that he was an exceedingly intelligent person.

Another day I went to pay him my return visit, and stumbled on a group of Kirghizzees who were in the act of carrying out a sentence of the Sultan's upon a man who had stolen a horse; according to the law of the Koran he had forfeited his life. The Sultan was alone persuaded to spare him by the elders of the tribe, in order that his grace might prove a favourable omen of his alliance with Russia, and of the success of the impending undertaking.

The Sultan granted his life for these reasons, and the offender was only scourged; this was effected in the following manner:—He was hunted from one side to another by two riders armed with whips, being himself fastened to the tail of a horse. At the conclusion of this ceremony, of which I was accidentally a witness, I presented myself to the Sultan, who was seated in the middle of a large round tent; his friends sat in a semi-circle on one side, and seats were placed for us on the other; a mixture of objects of luxury and of the first necessaries of life, as well as an ostentation of cleanliness with a costly taste and habit, were discernible. The walls were adorned with carpets, clothes hung upon a line, and tiger skins were outspread; whilst we distinguished, close to a rich diadem decorated with gold and costly stones, bits of meat suspended by a hook, as well as several wooden vessels and large skins filled with mare's milk.

On the journey from the Ilek to Tamby-i-aman we discovered on a hill large ammon's horns about four inches in circumference, as well as several large copper-yielding stones, which water had probably carried to this position. Not far from the mouth of the Suruk-Sir four small streams fall into Ilek, which, from this point, bears the name of Bechtomak, or "five rivers."

The road to the top of Bassaghi, from which one has a very extensive view, rises so suddenly that one is astonished to find oneself at last at so great a height; this hill is formed of a crystallized gypsum, with which in this part the whole steppe is interspersed. Its height would seem to reach about thirty toises; on the north-east its slope is very gentle. That on the south-east is, however, very steep, a singularity observable in nearly all hills as far as the Sir. Beyond the Bassaghi, the country is in general unproductive; the Kawal, or pasture land, which up to this point is luxuriant, becomes scanty, and only produces a few miserable plants in consequence of the excessive heat of the summer. We passed, by a ford, the Kubleili-temir, about three toises broad, and, in some places, about one toise deep, for which we had to have the ice cut with axes. I saw here a young Kirghizzee who had already been at work for ten minutes in the water, bring his axe to the bank, and then fearlessly return and dive three times—an unmistakable proof of the physical endurance and hardiness of this nomad tribe.

As I walked along the stream (which is there very interesting to a geognost on account of belemnites and skeletons of mice that are discovered in a steep mound about ten feet high, as well as for its narrow rows of pine, and its argillaceous conglomerate) and sought for valuable petrifactions, I saw suddenly in the air a large animal, which, springing from the mound alluded to, appeared as though it sought to hurl me over. I drew back, and it fell before my feet on the ice below, which it broke through, smashing its legs. It was a "Saiga," a description of antelope which the Cossacks hunt, and which, when pursued to steep precipices, is led to destroy itself through blind fear; this is a common habit of the Saigas, and often enough they thus hunt themselves and fall into the hands of the impassive Kirghizzee.

The Donish Cossacks catch them in this way: when, in the heat of the summer, herds of four or five thousand head come from the steppes and seek to swim the Don to reach cooler grazing grounds, they arm themselves with knives, and, plunging into the river, capture an enormous number of these animals. Credible people have assured me that, in the month of June, they have seen herds of these antelopes in the mountains of Guberlinsk, or the Aral, numbering 8,000 or 9,000 head. The flesh of the Saiga has a rich taste, and their skins furnish clothing; their horns are not, as one would expect, straight, but in the form of a lyre; the snout is usually bent, like that of a Kirghiz sheep, and is furnished with unusually large and deep nostrils, which possess a very elastic and soft cartilage.

When Saigas are young they can very easily be tamed, and, near Orenburg, one may see them following their masters about like dogs.

They are, besides, secured in many ways, especially when, during the summer heat, they seek shady places and lie in heaps of about twenty, the sunken head of each behind the belly of the one in advance, the foremost one having his head resting behind a stone or in a hole; at these times they are easily destroyed; the foremost one is killed, when the next one takes his place, and receives the blows of the hunter, who, in this manner, can kill several in a row.

From the Kubleili we went to the heights of Musscoil, which are similar to those of Bassaghi, and saw at a distance of 60 versts the mountains of Murghodjar, which raise themselves majestically, and afford a very artistic appearance with their bluish contours at the limit of the horizon. Nevertheless, we wished much to have them behind us, for the Kirghizzees say that the climate on the southern side is much milder; besides, we had been fortunate enough up to this point in having commonly enjoyed sunshine, and the thermometer only fell from 5° to 8° below zero. On one occasion only did it mark 10° (Reaumur), a cold which, whilst it appears in itself comparatively slight, is still sufficiently perceptible when one is seated the whole day in a tent of felt, without any of the requisites for a fire.

The Cara-a-Kenti, fifteen versts from the Murghodjar, has a deepening saline and muddy stream, impregnated with clay; in fact, the worst water that during this journey we were forced to drink. The Kirghizzees enjoyed the grimaces which we indulged in on account of its taste. We could scarcely make tea with it; the Kirghizzees came in crowds to drink tea; they commonly drink milk in bucketsful, and they introduce it into their tea with unbounded liberality.

I have seen several who have taken as much as eight pounds of this drink. I calculate by pounds because the vessels in which we poured the liquid held just about a pound of water.

CHAPTER III.

The Murghodjars; Airuk-tagh; the Sea of Aral; the Sir Daria.

On the 29th October we had reached the foot of the Murghodjars, whose highest peak bears the name of Airuk-tagh, "isolated mountain;" with good reason, for, with its height of about a half hundred toises, it raises itself very remarkably above the others. It is called "Airuruk," or fork, because it has two prongs. The Kirghizzees usually bestow very characteristic names upon objects which they learn to recognize: thus, for example, they call the hill lying to the south of the Airuk-tagh the Yaman-tagh, or "bad hill;" that lying to the north, Yokbehi-tagh, or the "good hill",—the first because it has little vegetation; the last because it possesses an abundance of pasture and water.

The Murghodjars, whose conical peaks and fantastic grouping present a romantic appearance, and in which porphyry, serpentine, quartz, and feldspar, but nowhere granite, are discovered, are plainly an off-shoot of the mountains of Suberlinsk: their connection is discovered between the foot of the mountains of that name and those of Orsk; here also it is that the Aral has forced for itself a bed through a chain of rocks and twists its way between steep and rocky banks.

These mountains have in the steppe the name Sasch Kitchu and Caraoul-tepeh.

At first separated by the Kir-Gheldi, they re-unite about 30 versts from the Aral, and appear, towards the south, to form the Urkatsch Mountains, or Mountains of the Ur, a river which waters their base.

The Urkatsch Mountains join the Murghodjars at the source of the river which flows to the south-west, while from the east two ranges of hills run to the west, one dividing the basin of the Aral from that of the Ilek, the other that of the Ilek from the Temir and the Emba.

The mountains of Yatchi-tagh follow the right bank of the Ur, and then, separating themselves from it, unite with those of Kamadur, which signifies "union of mountains."

The Murghodjars, the highest mountains of the steppe inhabited by small bands of Kirghizzees, are also a ramification of the Ural chain, from which, moreover, no branch throws itself out sufficiently prominently to reach the Altai. We passed the Murghodjars by a pass of six versts; they terminated at the bank of the Tuban, where we halted.

I have already mentioned the temperature which these mountains exhibit on the farther side; the snow falls no longer in large quantities, the climate is warmer, and the black soil indicates more traces of life and more vegetation; moreover, during a space of 400 versts from the Kaoundjur to the Sir, not a single river presents itself. The whole extent, in which are several salt lakes and broad plains, affords the most unmistakable evidence that it was formerly a sea bed from which the water has retired.

The first level which had offered itself to our sight stretched from the Tuban to the Kaoundjur, throughout which we only discovered water in a few hollows. In such a barren land every drop is of value, and the Kirghizzees never forget a spot which they have once in their lives visited. Thus, our principal guide, Emanschibey, who had not been in the neighbourhood for ten years, advised us to stop at a halting ground near the Kaoundjur, after a march of 20 versts, because he was confident that we should first encounter water at the Kodja Kul, a lake which was 15 versts distant; for the Kirghizzee, whose special duty it was to regulate our march, had repeatedly deluded us in this particular; we, nevertheless, set out, but the day drew to a close, and no sign of the lake could be observed, and at a season when the nights are especially dark it was particularly hard to set ourselves right, when once we had lost the way, on a steppe which exhibits no track and has no habitation. We could no longer trace our route by the form of the mountains or the tops of the hills, which the Kirghizzees are accustomed to employ as sign-posts, and without which it is easy to lose oneself. They advised us rather to attempt sleep than to wander hopelessly in search of water; as, however, it had already been determined that we should go to the lake previously mentioned, the march was accomplished under very many difficulties.

The Kirghizzees took every pains to keep on in the right direction, seeking with infinite trouble the smallest indications of a footpath, which in that place is usually a safe index to the direction of water. We had already advanced several hours in the darkness, and were under great apprehension that we had lost our way, when a Kirghizzee who had ridden a verst in advance attracted us by a discharge from his firelock, which, amongst them, is, at night-time, the signal that a horse has been stolen. He led us altogether about three versts to the banks of the Kodja Kul, after we had in that day put 45 versts behind us. This lake takes its name from the Kirghiz Kodja or Canton, which is separated from the rest by a pillar on the boundary. In the neighbourhood of the Sir these pillars are always more frequent and important, especially where they indicate a burial-ground, which has often the appearance of a town; they are usually constructed of clay, or potter's earth (terre glaise) mixed with cut straw, and partly with sun-burnt bricks. The Kodja Kul, whose bank is lined with shrubs, is very small in the autumn, but if the Kaoundjur pours itself into it, it has a considerable circumference. We quitted this lake in good time the following morning, and moved in the direction of the Cul-Kaduk, or "slave springs," which at the boundary of the desert of Vorzuk present a most striking appearance. This place is composed of shifting sand, which forms an immense number of small heaps of two or three toises high, which during every strong puff of wind alter their contouring completely. We had the greatest difficulty in making our way through this heavy sand, for our horses stumbled terribly on account of the bad footing it afforded.

On the 9th November we approached the hill Cara-Butak after having passed the Murghodjars, as well as the so-called Vorzuks. Sand hills or downs are met with in the neighbourhood of the Sea of Aral, as well as the larger Vorzuks: in the northern bank of this sea the first terminate, while the last spread themselves out between the Sea of Aral and the Caspian, and lose themselves at about 10 days' journey from Khiva: the ground is here invariably undulating and the hills terminate in gentle inclines. The Mug-Wort (artemesia) is the only plant which the horses can use as fodder, but at Adji-Kubuk we discovered a new kind of shrub termed Sak-Savul, which is highly valued by the Kirghizzees and other nomad tribes as fuel, because its cinders retain fire an entire day under ashes and afford a very pleasant warmth in a tent.

The Sir-Savul is a description of tamarisk, and bears leaves which are like those of the juniper tree: its bark is pea-yellow and its tough and hard wood is easily broken than cut. As far as the neighbourhood of the D'jan-Daria it is no more than two inches in diameter; beyond this point, however, it sometimes becomes a tree; it then attains a thickness of half a foot and a height of two toises, and spreads itself so persistently that it has the appearance of a regular thicket.

On the south side of the Cara-Butak I discovered a number of caves, and by a closer inspection of the ground near their entrance rows of mussels and shell-fish three or four feet thick. As I spoke to our Kirghizzees of this evidence of water in earlier times, they assured me that only in the time of their fathers the Sea of Aral stretched as far as the foot of the mountains of Cara-Butak, which are now about 60 versts distant. This assertion was established by such a number of Kirghizzees that I accept it as an indisputable and certain fact, which shows how considerably and how quickly the Sea of Aral is retiring, which formerly was, moreover, always advancing.

About 25 versts from Cara-Butak we had the Devman-bachi to our right, an isolated hill which may be seen a long way off, and which is named by the Kirghizzees "Termembes," and is thus called by their entire race, although it is often customary among them to give several names to the same place. Before we reached the Sea of Aral we came to the desert of Cara-cum, or "black sand," a distinction the reason of which I could not discover, for all these deserts appear to present a very similar appearance. The plain, which is provided with water more or less saline at two toises depth below its surface, extends to the Sea of Aral, and in some places as far as the Sir; it also runs on the east and widens itself greatly in that direction. On my return journey from Bokhara I took the line of this desert from the Sir to the Tighiz, a journey of eight days, and a distance of about 260 versts; we quitted

the desert of Cara-cum at Camechlu-bagh, a considerable bay or bend
which is formed by the Sir; it has a circuit of about 50 versts, and possesses for the most part the sweetest water which we met with throughout our entire journey.   The day after our arrival I made an excursion,
in company with several new comers and a few Cossacks, to inspect
the entrance of the Sir into the Sea of Aral, in this we succeeded,
after which we went round half the bay, and then rode some 20 versts
along the river.   Yet the Caraiar and the On-adem, which are a sort of
foreland near the mouth of the Sir, partly conceal the view of the Sea of
Aral.

At Camechlu-bagh and along the course of the Sir we encountered
a great number of Kirghizzees who had avoided the cold of the northern steppes and were in search of a milder climate; we stumbled among
some such whom the Khan had robbed of their flocks; necessity had
forced them to adopt fishing and agriculture, two pursuits which amongst
the Kirghizzees are held as evidence of poverty.   During 30 years have
both these half-savage people made war and plundered each other, partly
aggressively and partly by way of reprisals termed "Barranta."   As a
result of this unquietness they began to employ flour with their food,
this use and thrift has made already one of their principal necessities;
yet they use it sparingly, and prefer to buy it or barter sheep for it: they
send camels' hair to the frontier of Russia and so forth, in order that
they may be spared the trouble of tilling an unthankful soil.

They also dread being reduced by agriculture to the condition
of clods, while they consider that their happiness consists "in being free
as the birds of the air," a simile which they are always accustomed
to use if one speaks to them of their nomad life.   On this subject,
an old saying amongst them points out the result which would follow
from their building houses and adopting agriculture, a prophesy the
belief in which is strengthened amongst them by the example of the
Baschkirees, whose fate they fear.   Consequently, it is only the poorest
people who possess appliances for sowing the corn, which they cultivate
in some places near the Ilek, Emba, Tighiz, and Or, in the valleys of the
Murghodjars and Urkatsch, as well as near the Camechlu-bagh and the
Sir Daria, but particularly between the D'jan and the Kuwan-Daria, where
the Cara-Calpuks have only lived some 15 years.   They choose principally places in which the rain or snow-water has accumulated, and often
decline to give themselves the trouble of draining their fields by small
ditches, which neglect for example, in the neighbourhood of the Sir
and the Camechlu-bagh, results in ruin, they collect the water in cisterns
and irrigate those lands which lie naturally within a small circuit:
even near the Emba and Tighiz, where they save themselves this
laborious work, the fields are only a few poles square.   The Kirghizzees
usually cultivate millet, which yields a hundred-fold and thrives under all
conditions.   In the vicinity of the Sir there are ditches five or six
feet deep, which establish it as a fact that at some earlier period the
Kirghizzees had with labour achieved success in this work: here they
cultivate wheat and barley, the first of which they reap in autumn,
the second in spring; their crops they store in small burrows under
the ground.

On the 19th November the embassy had accomplished a march
of 41 days, and reached the bank of the Sir Daria opposite the height of

Carateph; during the last 15 versts we entered upon a plain bearing shrubs, and here and there luxuriant grass, which stretches as far as 80 versts from the mouth of the Sir, and is from 10 to 15 versts broad.

Beyond this plain, which in spring is commonly flooded, one distinguishes the sand tracts of Cara-cum, which extend right up to the Sir, and for a 150 versts further along its course. The Cara-cum, which is rich in water, is, during the winter, usually inhabited by the Kirghizzees, who with their kibitkas endeavour to find shelter from the wind in the hollows. At the Sir Daria, the common place of resort for the poor, necessity has multiplied the number of robbers, and we often saw Kirghizzees on the hills who appeared to be looking out for a straggler or a horse. Our guide called our attention to them, and every one was in consequence on his guard. Near its mouth the Sir is about 60 toises broad; 15 versts further up, however, it spreads itself over 120 toises. It is rapid and navigable, at any rate from Kokan downwards. Several of the Kirghizzees told us that it was fordable at a distance of about 130 versts from its mouth, though only during the extreme heat of summer; others, however, disclosed that this is not so.

CHAPTER IV.

Customs, usages, and character of the Kirghizzees.

The spots watered by the Sir represent the paradise of the steppe to the Kirghizzees, who are proud to possess so great a river in their territory. Their chief desire is to be able to winter with their flocks upon its banks, where the cold is not even so severe as upon those of the Ilek, or Tighiz, or upon the Murghodjar or Urkatsch Mountains, or in the sand plains of the Cara-cum. The wealthy Kirghizzees had been prevented, during six years, from spending their winters in these milder spots, because their enemies the Khivans used to plunder them directly an opportunity presented itself. The Kirghizzees like to reside amongst reeds, which are thick and strong enough to afford a protection against the tempest. These nomads appear, as a rule, to be inclined to melancholy, and consequently affect a liking for the roar of the waves of the Sir; they often spend half the night seated on a rock, contemplating the moon and improvising sorrowful rhymes, for which their airs are not a little melancholy.

They have also epics, in which they sing the heroic deeds of their forefathers and heroes: only these songs are sung by professional bards, and I could scarcely hear any of them. I often begged our Kirghizzees to sing me some of their national songs; but they usually improvised verses relating to certain persons or events that had little poetic merit. One day I heard a youthful Kirghizzee sing the song of a young maiden, which may be interpreted somewhat as follows :—

"Do you see yonder snow? Go to!

"My body is whiter;

"Do you see the blood of yonder slaughtered sheep? Go to!

"My cheeks are more red;

"Climb up yonder hill; you will see the burnt stem of a tree. Go to!

"My hair is darker;

"The Sultan has Mollahs who write much. Go to!

"My eyebrows are blacker than their ink."

Another sang me the following:—"See the Aoul (group of tents), which belongs to a very rich man; he has only a solitary daughter; in the day she remains at home, and at night she goes out walking, and has only the moon as her companion."—A third, a Kirghiz Beg, rich and the head of a numerous family, improvised his thoughts thus: "A poor but brave Beg is of more value than a despicable Khan," whereupon he puffed his checks out significantly as though he were an acknowledged enemy of the Khan of the Kirghizzees.

These staves can, to a certain extent, convey a notion of the poetical ideas of the Kirghizzees, those children of the desert who, with the exception of religion, have remained free from every influence of foreign civilization and afford a true picture of a nomad people that loves independence of everything and despises whatever prejudices their freedom. Frank and free, warlike and bold, a Kirghizzee all alone on his horse in the desert dares and accomplishes a journey of 500 or 600 versts with inconceivable rapidity in order to seek a friend or a relative amongst foreign hordes. On his road he enters each encampment in which he stops; he tells the news and shares in the repast of his hosts, quite sure to find welcome, though they do not know him at all. This meal usually consists of " Krut" (a sort of cheese), which is also known in Persia, Afghanistan, and Bokhara, further of Hairan (sheep and goat's milk which has turned somewhat sour), meat, and, where possible, of Kumes, a drink manufactured with mare's milk, which is highly prized in the deserts. A Kirghizzee never forgets a place where he has been before, and after some days of absence travels back with new matter to relate, to discuss his journey in the bosom of his family.

His wives are obliged, all of them, to perform some handiwork; they have not only to attend to the cooking, but must also make his clothes and saddle his horse, whilst he in uninterrupted indolence only undertakes calmly to watch the sheep. I have seen the brother of a Sultan on horseback grazing his sheep, occupying himself in this manner for several weeks without having in the least sacrificed his dignity.

The Kirghizzees are governed by so-called elders or heads of families, as well as by Begs, Behadirs, Sultans, and Khans.

The title of Beg is a purely honorary one; only he who cannot maintain it by personal worth and character soon loses it, while the man who attracts attention increases its value, so that by degrees it becomes the custom to call him "Sultan," or that this distinguished name is conferred upon him by a body of his associates. An "elder of elders" is usually an old man, whose advice they are accustomed to follow: he must, moreover, be rich and have a numerous family, because these things, together with good intelligence, are the necessaries for being able to rule these tribes.

The "Behadirs" are Kirghizzees of acknowledged bravery and spirit of enterprise, who serve in war-time as partizans. "Sultans" are the relatives of the Khans, and nearly always possess considerable influence amongst the Kirghizzees; they also have the title of "Tura" or Lord, but they must also have personal worth if they wish to secure the submission of the people. The Khan has with the Kirghizzees the power of life and death; they have no other appeal from his despotism than public opinion: this opinion is, however, with these nomad races of trifling importance, because discontented members often separate themselves from one Chief and choose another. Yet the Khan is forced to observe custom or established precedent, as well as not to act in opposition to the laws of the Koran. This last point more especially affects his authority, so he is careful to secure a Mollah completely devoted to him, who states its laws according to his interests, and interprets in the most agreeable way for the Khan the passages of the sacred volume, which, for the most part, have a double signification; by means of which the Chief succeeds in carrying out much which, without it, he would be unable to accomplish. He is also accustomed to surround himself with a council of men, for the most part old, who appear to enjoy popularity amongst the Kirghizzees; their devotion he endeavours to secure by flattery or generosity.

All these precautionary measures do not, however, serve to assure him his authority over his immediate subjects unless he is able to make himself beloved by them in consequence of his prowess, daring, and courage; his power too is based on a common consent that he will not act contrary to the national interest: when he has once secured this, he is firmly established and can rule despotically. Public opinion in this respect is carried along with his power, but he must win it over to himself in order to rule. Whoever postponed or treated this people with scorn would bring it about, that the very power which occasioned his elevation would effect his ruin.

The Kirghizzees are very vindictive and hasty in temper; the slightest thing, often the disappointment of some trivial expectation, succeeds in putting them into a horrible passion. Warred upon for many years by the Khivans, they sought assistance from the Bokharians, whose caravans the former had plundered on every occasion. They hoped in consequence that the Government of Bokhara would make common cause with them; deceived in this expectation they became enraged, and determined on their part to take the first opportunity of robbing the Bokharian caravans. One of their petty Chiefs cut the tail off his horse and took it to the chief Vizir at Bokhara, making use of these words— " As the tail is cut off from my horse, I cut myself off from you, and will in future become your implacable foe."

He disappeared immediately with the two or three friends who accompanied him, and carried off five camels and two Bokharians in proof of the declaration of war which he had singly offered to the whole of Bokhara.

Robbery is as deeply engrained in the disposition of these tribes as vindictiveness; it is especially prevalent amongst the largest and smallest of the Kirghizzee tribes, whilst those of a medium size, who for the last century have been better governed, are accustomed to enjoy regular quiet and peacefulness. Their warlike habits and indifference to hardships upon long expeditions, and especially the influence which religious fanaticism has over this rough people, assure their Chiefs a large following in any bold undertaking. It is also observable that these nomads prefer to unite during a hard winter, from which they have much to suffer, in order to undertake a warlike expedition or to establish themselves in a country which enjoys a milder climate; notably in Bokhara, which is famous with them, and in comparison with their wastes is so beautiful. In this manner these wanderings of the barbarians can continually be renewed in a country little practicable for artillery, and which possesses few regular troops. I close this digression upon the Kirghizzees with the remark that they never call themselves by this name; they term themselves Kazaks, which word with some signifies Emperor (Reichter), with others warrior. I beg to say that they have received the name of Kirghizzees from the Baschkirees, but they do not know the origin of it, which also is only bestowed upon the nomads of the larger tribes. These last acknowledge no Khan as their Chief, but are under several Sultans, who at one time seek the protection of Russia and at another that of China, and offer presents with this object. The Kirghizzees of the principal tribe, so called, more especially fear the Chinese, whose bad and often cruel politics, with reference to them especially, are justified by necessity.

Once upon a time, when a caravan was plundered on the frontier of Sungaria, which was watched by outposts of Mandschies, the Chinese made use of reprisals, and a thousand Kirghizzees guilty or not paid for this attack with their lives.

Several examples of this kind point to the destruction of the Kirghizzees who live on the borders of the Chinese Empire.

In both the other tribes, the Khans are obliged to be recognized in their dignity by Russia, which also exercises a great influence over their election: they are also obliged to tender the oath of allegiance; just as the Khans of Khiva and Bokhara demand a tribute from the Turcomans, the Kirghizzees are tributaries of Russia, but we are first bound to afford them protection against the Khivans, and to prove to them in this manner the value of a protection the full importance of which they soon enough recognize and appreciate.

CHAPTER V.

In the month of June the melted snow from the Abbatagh swells the water of the Sir Daria, which overflows its banks and floods and fertilizes the adjacent country, so that the soil with a small expenditure of labour yields corn, fruit, pasturage, and plane trees, as well as perhaps cotton and mulberries. At the time of our journey, however, this river was frozen, and we had to cross it with the greatest possible care, for the ice was so weak that it broke under the weight of our two guns. One camel fell through with his load, and was only saved with infinite pains. The Kirghizzees strewed rushes and scattered ashes upon the ice to prevent the camels from slipping. At length, after many complications and anxieties, we all crossed in safety the Sir, which, in ancient times, was celebrated as the Yasartes! (Yaxartes)—

On our return journey in April our passage of the same river was much more difficult and tedious, for we occupied two days in effecting it. Our two vessels were obliged to be formed into a raft, on which the artillery and troops found a place: three large but tolerably fragile boats belonging to the Kirghizzees carried our baggage over for a trifling sum.

The horses and camels were obliged to swim; it was a wonderful sight to see these last tied in dozens, one behind the other, accompanied by the Kirghizzees, who, showing off to advantage the athletic frames of their naked bodies, at one time kept themselves close to these creatures, at another swam by their sides and encouraged them by shouting. The bodies of three of the camels which were drowned were dragged on shore turned towards Mecca, and with the customary prayers the entrails were cut out, which the drivers instantly devoured. When a camel is swimming, it lays itself on one side, to secure a larger surface and to support itself by its humps, which lie horizontally on the surface of the water. In the vicinity of the Sir, we passed through a plain furnished with rushes, and in some places with water, which forced us to make several detours; the Kurwan Daria, an arm of the Sir (from 10 to 15 toises broader, and from 5 to 10 feet deeper,) which flowed along our route for four days, winds its limpid waters between the sand heaps which extend as far as the D'jan-Daria. On our road back from Bokhara we struck the banks of the Aralu-Kullars, a row of lakes which stretch along the Kuwan to the point where the D'jan-Daria cuts itself off. Some of these are 10 versts in circumference; others are merely small hollows filled with water, which dry up in summer, and are then deepened by the Kirghizzees. This is the least unfruitful part which I saw in the steppe: traces of large fields are here discovered, which the Cara-Calpuks cultivated still in the year 1806. This tribe, of Calmuck origin, from their poverty and weakness, were unable to withstand the repeated onslaughts of the Kirghizzees; in the year 1740 they called for the help of the Russian Government as well as that of the Khivans, and even the Bokharians, in consequence of the refusal of which they left in the year 1807 their fruitful fields, and, in the hope of a more peaceful fate, submitted themselves to the Khivans and Bokharians. Divided in this way the Cara-Calpuks still wander about, some to the south of the Sea of Aral, others westward from Samarcand and north of the Zerafschan: as they are very poor and only possess a few camels, they use two-wheeled carts, which are drawn by oxen and horses.

The D'jan-Daria is, on either side, adjoined by an argillaceous plain, which was, once upon a time, broken up with sand-hills, which are connected with the sand plains of Kinoan or of the Kizil-Kum. Thickets of the previously mentioned Sak-Savul tree are discovered in these plains, in which several wild beasts, the wolf for example, wild-cats, and even tiger, conceal themselves: many of the Kirghizzees assured me that they were obliged to remove their flocks from this neighbourhood, in order not to expose them to the danger of being stolen by these voracious animals, which they dare not attack when they are united, but only when they become isolated. As a final measure about 20 men armed with guns and matches arrange a species of drive: they surround the reeds in which the tiger has established himself, and set fire to them on the windward side; the heat and the flames compel him to leave his haunt, and expose himself to the bullets of the hunters. We employed similar means upon the banks of Aralu-Kuar and the Kurwan Daria, in whose rush thickets a great crowd of wild pig exist; of these we killed, amongst other things, 18 in a short day of three hours: this description of hunting affords a very pleasant spectacle. Large volumes of smoke rose from the midst of the burning thicket in the middle of the plain; we saw through the flames a hundred Cossacks, who with slack bridles and clutching thighs galloped here and there to right and left, whilst our horses carried us sometimes forward, sometimes backward, and very near the wild pig, which entangled themselves in the morass, and very soon sank, just as quickly appearing again.

On all sides one heard shots from pistols and flint-locks; here lay wounded horses which the Kirghizees purchased in order to eat them, there raging Cossacks stormed at the wild pig endeavouring to run them through with their pikes; one Cossack officer of the Jaik, enraged that the Kirghizees had offered him assistance, sprang from his horse and attacked a horribly big wounded boar, pulled him by the ears, and discharged a pistol bullet through his brain.

I can scarcely give the reader an idea of the joy which I experienced when I found myself once more in a wood; the roaring of the wind through the branches, the quivering of the leaves of the trees, the greenness of the landscape, all this seemed to me as something entirely new, recalled to me the memories of my father-land, and raised in me the most pleasurable sensations. Amongst these deserts and with these nomads one first learns to appreciate the good fortune of being a European.

We saw in these plains traces of irrigation which indicated that in former times the country was more thickly populated than now; moreover, in the Kirghizee Steppe no place is seen in which traces of habitations in former times are more frequent than on the banks of the D'jan-Daria. I saw the ruins of Kul-Tschuktam; this mass of upheaped earth or walls, which extend to a distance of about 150 toises, and the highest of which is 3 toises high, is easily seen to indicate that the ancient dwellings were built of brick; traces of irrigation canals, which were one toise broad and 2 feet deep, are found, as well as pots and vessels: the ruins are situated at 15 versts from the D'jan-Daria. The Kirghizees can, moreover, afford no more extended information with respect to this place than that it was inhabited by the Nogais, with which name they speak of the former inhabitants of their steppe, whilst the Baschkirees also call their forefathers by the same. One observes that very many ruins exist in the open part of the country, and that they are usually discovered in the neighbourhood of the Tobol, the Ilek, and the Emba. Those which are considered the most important and best of all are those of Djan-Kend, which commonly have been accepted as the residence of the Chief of the Ouz.

The D'jan-Daria is probably the ancient Kizil-Daria, in which it is possible that the former flowed, entering it further southwards, for, 40 versts to the south, we discovered the bed of a large stream: but the D'jan-Daria itself, which scarcely ten years ago, was of a considerable size, and even in 1816 exceeded the Kuwan in breadth, has lately become only a dried-up bed more than a 100 toises broad; banks from 3 to 4 toises high, and a number of pools from 2 to 3 toises deep, only a few of which hold water at all seasons, these are the only traces of the stream which no longer exist. This sudden drying up astonished our Kirghizees much, because they could not explain the cause of it. Some of them ascribed it to the circumstance that the water of the D'jan-Daria had been turned off by a dam at the position where it separates itself from that river in order to irrigate the fields on the bank of the Kuwan; others declare, with more probability, that the D'jan-Daria has been choked by the sand of the Kizil-Kum: perhaps, however, one may attribute this decrease of the waters to their tendency to dissipate by evaporation. Whatever may be the cause, the fact is sure and undeniable that this great river is dried up; the water which is discovered in the hollows of its ancient bed tastes slightly of sulphur; it is the most unhealthy which we met with on our journey, and has the more unpleasant results that it is impossible to replace it by any other during five days in the desert of Kizil-Kum, through which the road to Bokhara lies. Our soldiers suffered from cholic from its use, and some from a strong griping, whilst one of them died in convulsions. When we left the D'jan-Daria on the 3rd December we entered the main road to Bokhara. I call it so because it is three toises broader, and, on account of the crowd of passengers, is always much travelled: in the first place it winds itself through a wood of Sak-Saouls, and is then scarcely visible in an argillaceous plain which extends 57 versts from the D'jan-Daria, but is again much frequented at the Kizil-Kum, where it passes through the valleys formed by the sand-hills. This road is much used by all caravans from Bokhara which go to Orsk or to Orenburg, as well as by all the Kirghizees who drive cattle from the market of Bokhara to the open portion of the steppe: they take pains to traverse the Kizil-Kum at the narrowest possible place, and to provide themselves with water from the celebrated well of Bukhan, which lies upon its southern boundary.

The D'jan-Daria makes a division in the land between Orenburg and Bokhara: the soil on that side is argillaceous, but more productive, because of the heat of the climate; it rests upon a basis of clay, whilst the steppe of the Kirghizees is formed either of sand or limestone.

The climate also affords a great difference: (tortoises) land turtle, which are seldom met with to the north of the D'jan-Daria, are frequently found in the Kizil-Kum; a small amount of snow falls there, which never lies long; in a word, everything points to a warmer climate. The banks of the Kuwan and the D'jan-Daria, especially in the neighbourhood of the Sea of Aral, are inhabited by Kirghizees, who pay tribute to the Khivans; the dryness of the soil is remarkable; from the D'jan-Daria to the cultivated districts, a space of 500 versts, one does not meet with a single river and with water only in the more or less easily discovered wells, which, throughout this extent, contain for the most part salt water.

In the direction in which we crossed it the Kizil-Kum is 100 versts broad; its length is very considerable, for it extends from the Sir-Daria, where it is very broad, to the Sea of Aral and the Amoo-Daria. This desert is even remarkable for its arid nature; springs are nowhere met with. They declare that formerly three wells existed near the route which we adopted, but that they have been filled up to prevent them from being useful to the robbers, who usually lie concealed behind the neighbouring sand-hills : these robbers have, in fact, been driven away, but at present they collect in the hollows of the hills of Bukhan, from which, if they feel themselves strong enough, they sally out, fall upon, and plunder the travellers who are passing, or even kill them in case of resistance.

The wells of Bukhan are in consequence as dangerous as were formerly those of Kizil-Kum, and doubtless all the more that this part of the road between Bokhara and Orenburg lies closest to Khiva, and the Khivans are often engaged in war either with the Kirghizees or the Bokharians, or even, as in 1820, with both at once. We were in consequence thoroughly on our guard, and sent forward patrols into the defiles of the hills of Bukhan, and fortunately we safely traversed these dangerous places; but 10 days after us a caravan of Bokharians and Kirghizees was plundered by the Khivans, who fell upon them from an ambush near the wells of Bukhan and followed the fugitives as far as the Kizil-Kum, where they met a body of Kirghizees, with whom they engaged in a combat. On our return journey we found more than 100 corpses exposed to the attack of dogs and birds which were near that place. Fragments of porcelain and delf, broken cases, and here and there metal vessels, scattered over the sand, marked the spot where the fugitives were overtaken and killed to a man. The Kizil-Kum is furnished here with little sand-hills, which for the most part stand four and ten toises above the plain, but the Bech-tepeh, or the five heights, are about 30 toises high; these are situated by the route which we pursued. From the summit of the highest of them the eye wanders over a boundless superficies which resembles a storm-driven sea that has been suddenly converted into sand. We searched in vain to discover an object upon which the eye could fasten; nothing is observable, but a vast, sad, and uniform wilderness, and only a few shrubs, some prickly bushes, in the autumn no grass, and in spring so sparing a vegetation that it is soon dried up and changes into dust. Of living creatures one discovers in this desert, spite of its aridity, a number of lizards of all sorts, chameleons, tortoises, rats, woodpeckers (?), hawks (vultures ?), and a number of birds of a bluish plumage, which we did not see again in the spring; they resembled crows; only in size they were much smaller.

The basis of the Kizil-Kum is clay of a reddish colour, which in some places is observable protruding from the sand, hence the origin of the name of this desert, for Kizil signifies red, and Kum sand. As soon as one has left the bank of the D'jan-Daria, one enters upon a boundless uninhabited extent, which stretches to within 40 versts of Bokhara and reaches Turkistan and Tashkend, as well as the banks of the Sir. This space, which comprises 8° or 9° of breadth, separates Bokhara from the Kirghizee Steppe and the Khanate of Kokhan from that of Khiva.

To the north of Bokhara a habitable land is met with, but fear of the Khivans, a cruel and daring people, prevents any one from settling there. Moreover, Bokhara itself possesses excellent pasturages there, and every year a number of Kirghizee families, especially the poor ones, leave their country in order to settle down in the wastes of Bokhara, whose peaceable, quiet condition and mild climate promise them a more happy fate.

From the D'jan-Daria forwards we traversed, as I have already remarked, a much-travelled way. Almost every day we met Kirghizee caravans which came from Bokhara, and, having sold their sheep, returned with barley, millet, tobacco, clothes, and woollen stuffs. It gave us great pleasure to converse with these "Bazartschis," as market-going people are called, to ask them the news of Bokhara, and to acquaint ourselves with the time of their departure from that capital. We were highly delighted to see ourselves nearly at the end of so wearisome and anxious a journey, which had begun to be very burdensome to us. Throughout the Kizil-Kum we accomplished every day from 42 to 46 versts, a very unusual distance, for we had to wade through sand; but it was absolutely necessary to hasten in order not to suffer from the great dearth of water. Our horses, which only found a very poor description of fodder in these deserts, fell off perceptibly, and the horses of the Baschkirees were so enfeebled they could no longer draw the six waggons which now remained of the 25 we had brought from Orenburg, the remainder we had burnt; we were forced to relieve them by the Cossack horses, which, till now, had carried our baggage: our entire community had, besides, become very thin, especially the infantry soldiers. We had lost several pack-horses, though no riding horses, notably once, when during one day 8 were unable to follow us for lack of strength. In one word, it was high time that we reached the end of our journey.

From the D'jan-Daria to Tuz-Kuduk, or "the five wells," it is 211 versts (51 French miles), which we hurried over in five days with our artillery, through a sandy desert destitute of water and pasturage, having previously accomplished, with the greatest possible celerity, a march of over 1,000 versts.

CHAPTER VI.

Tuz-Kuduk. Aghatma. Triumphant entry into Bokhara!

Having once passed the Kizil-Kum the traveller enters upon a plain about forty versts in length, completely covered with the absinth flower; it is bordered on the right by the mountains of Bukhan. The Bokharians who were accompanying us were so afraid of being attacked by Khivans, that they persuaded us to avoid the dangerous "wells of Bukhan" by giving us the idea of taking the shortest route to Tuz-Kuduk across this plain. This prevented us from making a closer inspection of the mountains of Bukhan, and I was unable to accomplish my wish until the next spring on our way back. They rise like the Murghodjar-Tag, about one hundred toises above the level of the plain; they are very steep, perforated with holes or caves; they consist chiefly of quartz, syenite, and diabese, and form a great many narrow passes. A small stream has its source in these mountains, and, passing close to the wells of Bukhan, winds its way into the plain for about a hundred toises, and then suddenly disappears.

Having crossed the above-mentioned plain, one enters a mountainous country in which are found the mountain chains of Bukhan, Tuz-Kuduk, Kapkantasch, &c., but which in themselves are nothing but the smaller offshoots of those large mountain ranges which run south of the Khanate of Kokhan and to the east of Bokhara. Near to the "wells of

Bukhan" the mountain chain begins to take a westerly direction, and continues until it reaches the banks of the River Amoo, thus forming the Mountains Tschavaswali and Vasilkara, which are celebrated on account of their gold mines, and which also, rumour says, were the principal motives for sending the expedition under Prince Bekewitsch; and it is even now the case that the Khan of Khiva forbids these mines being worked, so as not to excite the covetousness of the Russians. But I dare say, perhaps, these reports greatly exaggerate the wealth of these mountains, for in Orenburg I saw a bit of sulphuric stone (Sulphuret of Pyrites), which had been found in the Vasilkara Mountains, and there is no doubt that these productions have to a great extent misguided the inhabitants, who would look upon any piece of yellow mineral, interspersed with bits of sparkling metal, as gold.

The mountains which we now traversed consisted of either syenite and diabese or of quartz and chalk mixed, and were rounder shaped, and not so conically formed as the Murghodjars. The soil, that of the valleys, is less fertile, and even the absinth is here seldom seen. In some few places the road is very narrow, but otherwise broad and very good. Tuz-Kuduk, or "the five wells," is a narrow vale, in which are found two wells about three toises deep, and about thirty smaller ones mostly dried up. The mountainous district commences about seven versts on this side of Tuz-Kuduk and on the road to Aghatma. It continues thus for thirty-seven versts, as far as Kapkantasch, where we entered another plain, leaving the hills Bech-bulak and Buk-bulduk on our left. This name Buk-bulduk means in our language the same as nightingale, and is a sound which the Kirghizees have made to imitate the note of this bird.

In the neighbourhood of Kapkantasch are several springs of sulphuric, putrid, and exceptionally saline water, which our horses could hardly manage to drink.

The sandy plains of Butkak-Kum begin about twenty-two versts from Kapkantasch, and continue in the same direction for 27 versts more, of which the last four versts only are deep sand; 26 versts from this desert, we once more reached a mountainous district called Sooziz-kara, i.e., "black without water." These barren rocks have, indeed, a black appearance, and water is only found in two wells, which we left about ten versts to our left. Our provision of water having run out, we used snow as a substitute, of which we found plenty, and although these hills are of but small elevation, still we found the difference of temperature considerable. At last we reached Kara-aghatsch, after having, during the last four versts, traversed an unbroken plain, in itself perfectly even, but surrounded by mountains of considerable height.

At a distance of about two versts the embassy was met by four Bokharian Custom-house officers, who, going through the usual form of greeting " Be welcome," Khoosh-ameded, informed us that their Sovereign the Khan of Aghatma, which Khanate was still 38 versts off, had ordered provisions, &c., to be furnished for us. Herr Von Negri expressed our thankfulness, and we continued the rest of the journey to Kara-aghatsch in their company.

It was here for the first time that we once more saw trees. About a hundred very old mulberry trees surrounded a sulphur spring, the heat of which was certainly quite fifteen degrees Reaumur. A Mahomedan devotee had had these trees planted, in the shade of which he had passed his life and was buried. This spring juts out from a hill of clay, and the natives attribute a wonderful power to it. All the Mahomedans in our retinue bathed in it.

A number of rags and pieces of cloth or linen are seen hanging from the boughs of these trees; they are gifts offered to the memory of the devotee, who is buried at their foot. The water of this spring, which flows in good quantity, forms a small rivulet, but which, being sucked in by the clayey substance of the earth over which it runs, after a short distance totally disappears. Although we had marched for the last four days without a lengthened halt, still we commenced our march again on the fifth day, so as to leave this barren country as soon as possible, and the sooner to receive the provisions which the Khan had so kindly prepared for us.

We reached Aghatma on the 25th December after crossing a tolerably high mountain at Kara-aghatsch. The Bokharians declared that in former times a city had stood here, and a heap of remains of bricks, which is in existence, seems to prove this. Aghatma lies in a sort of funnel where one expects to discover the traces of a lake, from which probably the inhabitants of the city procured water: two abundant springs are found in the neighbourhood, whose sulphuric water is slightly warm, as that of Kara-aghatsch.

We noticed at Aghatma a small tower with a vaulted roof, which the Bokharians use as a kind of breast-work or outpost, in which they maintain a detachment of soldiers, either if they fear an attack from the Khivans or expect the arrival of a Russian caravan. A sentry posted on the top can survey the country for a great distance round. Before we reached Aghatma a Bokharian Yuz-bachi, or Commander of a hundred men, approached us with a following of about 20 riders, and informed the ambassadors that he was commissioned by the Khan to offer us whatever provisions might be necessary for us. Afterwards several mounted men approached Herr Von Negri, gave him their hand in oriental fashion, and welcomed him with an oft-repeated "Khoosh-ameded."

The greater part of their horses were very beautiful, large, swift, fiery, and went like lightning. The costume of these soldiers had no uniformity except in the wearing of a white turban. Each of them had a khalaat, that is, a large, broad overcoat, which varies in colour and material. Some wore it of striped silk, some of cloth, and others of a web of camel's hair, or they were furnished with a sort of woollen blouse which scarcely reached beyond the girdle. We obtained in Aghatma bread, fresh and white, splendid bunches of grapes, water-melons, and pomegranates. It is easy to imagine the pleasure that each of us experienced in disposing of this bread and fruit, if it is remembered that we had been obliged to live upon nothing but rusks for 70 days, and that these each day became harder. Our horses received good hay and ozugera: this last, which is given to horses in the place of oats, consists of a sort of white grain of the size and shape of linseed. Long since pasturage had failed, and even the absinth plants had become rare, and on this account our horses had become thin; the hay which was given them in Aghatma came from cultivated pastures, than which, especially in Bokhara, no better are known. Our horses were no longer accustomed to it, and many of them became ill, because they ate too much, or also, perhaps, in consequence of their being watered more than once a day, a practice the Bokharians never adopt when they feed their horses on hay: we lost 50 head in Bokhara, without doubt, chiefly in consequence of the sudden ending of the scant of their allowance, as on account of the duration of their fatigues.

Advancing from Aghatma we entered a plain which seemed to me to elevate itself imperceptibly towards the cultivated land: this plain is argillaceous, and on the road which we pursued towards Odun-Kuduk its surface is in a very few places covered with sand; we found much more on the road lying some versts to the westward, which we adopted on our way back. At Odun-Kuduk we observed the marks of old ditches and the ruins of a house, which appeared to indicate that formerly the cultivated portion of Bokhara stretched further to the north than at present, and that the boundary on this side was as now Kaghatan, seventeen versts from Odun-Kuduk. We counted about 100 paces between two rows of sand hills, under which we saw the ruins of walls and dwellings lying about; beyond this, to our extreme wonder, we entered an entirely different country, so much so that we imagined ourselves to be 1,000 miles away from the uniform space through which we had pushed for 70 days.

The desert ended at these hills: beyond we were surrounded by fields, ditches, and avenues; we saw on all sides houses, villages, fruit and vegetable gardens, mosques, and minarets; in a word, we fancied ourselves suddenly transported to fairy-land.

If the appearance of this country arouses a feeling of wonder amongst Europeans who are accustomed to see fruitful fields and populous places, what an impression must it not make upon the Kirghizees and the other inhabitants of the desert? How can they restrain themselves from invading a country so highly favoured by nature, which offers them in summer boundless pasturages for their nomad herds, and in winter towns and villages in which they can find shelter and defence against the intolerably hard climate? We found ourselves in a country almost entirely unknown to Europeans, in which everything excited our inquisitiveness, and it is easy to perceive with what interest we viewed the thousands of Orientals dressed in blue dresses and white turbans, who, some on foot, some on horses or donkeys, pressed forwards to see us and salute us in their peculiar oriental fashion. Several showed their pleasure in a forcible manner by coming close up to us and speaking a few coherent words in Russian; their signs of astonishment, their shouts and yells, and, lastly, the violent manner in which they struggled to get a stare at us, gave our entry into Bokhara the semblance of a popular ceremony, by which we would have been highly amused, if the presence of the Bokharian Police, whose voices were louder than the shouts of the crowd, and whose arms were dealing out blows to right and left in order to make room for us, had not reminded us that it was our entry that caused so much tumult, and that the longing to stare at Russians outweighed the annoyance of receiving blows. We were very much pained at seeing mixed up with this crowd of Asiatics a few poor Russian soldiers who had unfortunately fallen into slavery; most of them were weak, old men. On-recognizing their countrymen they could not refrain from tears; they stammered a few words in their mother-tongue and tried by every means to make way through the crowd to approach us : great was their delight at making our acquaintance. I cannot properly describe this touching scene, which tore my heart asunder.

At Khatun-Kuduk we heard that the Koosh-beghi, one of the most important officials of Bokhara, was awaiting us in the next village. About one verst from the cultivated land a Pendya-basho, *i.e.*, a commander of 500 men, met us with about 200 riders; he conducted us through the crowd, and our infantry with beating drums marched towards the tent in which the Koosh-beghi resided. About 30 toises from it we dismounted, and proceeded between two rows of foot soldiers, who were seated on the ground, but sprang to their feet the moment the ambassador passed them : we perceived several tents of different colours, at the pegs of which a great many richly caparisoned horses with gold embroidered saddle cloths were tied by their heads and hind feet. Many slaves and officials surrounded these tents, and everything we saw contributed to the *eclât* of this first meeting.

At the time Herr Von Negri entered the tent, the Koosh-beghi, whose name was Hakim Beg, was sitting in his tent, while close to him were four Bokharian grandees. He said to the suite of the embassy—" Be seated, for you are strangers; it gives me great pleasure to see you." Herr Von Negri then began to ask him about the ceremonies to be observed during the presentation to the Khan, but, unfortunately, the Koosh-beghi and he could not agree; in other respects this audience commenced under favourable auspices, but before it had ended the genuine Bokharian character exhibited itself. The Koosh-beghi was indiscreet enough to request Herr Von Negri to present the Khan with our two field-pieces, but seeing that he was not going to give them up, he, without circumlocution, asked Herr Von Negri for his own carriage, although he knew we had several camels laden with presents for the Khan. Hakim Beg appeared to be in about his 50th year; his long dark-brown beard was turning grey : he was of great stature; his face was prepossessing and good-natured-looking ; he spoke Persian with great fluency : as a turban, he wore a white Cashmere shawl and a cloak of the same material covered with large flowers, and a sable fur covered with striped Cashmere.

Our journey had turned out as fortunately as we could have wished ; with the exception of a few cloudy days, as well as a few hours of sleet and rain, the weather had been so entirely propitious that the Kirghizees declared that there must, without doubt, have been a " holy man" of the party : this continuance of clear weather favoured our journey very much, as it spared us all the discomfort which rain, cold, and snow might have inflicted. On the 17th December we passed the night in the small town of Waskend, for we had reached a very populous neighbourhood and a well-built place. We saw one not less pleasant-looking, on the following day, on our road to Bazarschi, a large village situated two versts from Bokhara. We had traversed 40 versts since our interview with the Koosh-beghi, and were, during these two days, closely attended by an exceptionally large crowd.

The Police hunted them incessantly by the way with strokes of their whips, but curiosity made them bear the blows patiently, run away, and come back again. Our soldiers marched in perfect order, in full uniform ; the roll of drums caused loud outcries of astonishment, and the Bokharians followed us with continual expressions of delight.

In the neighbourhood of Waskend four Bokharian gentlemen came to make their obeisance to Herr Von Negri, and also to present him with a congratulatory address from the Khan.

One of these was a relation of the Prince, but he could not speak Persian; he was the only one amongst the Usbeks, whom I saw, who could not speak the language.

About 15 versts from Bokhara the Commander of the Khan's Yassoots appeared, accompanied by 30 of his own men; he came to salute the ambassador, and he went with us as far as Bazarschi, in which place we also halted at a country-house of the Koosh-beghi; but the rooms were so damp that we preferred remaining in our tents, although we should much have liked to have parted company with them. After a discussion which lasted 36 hours over the formalities to be observed, an agreement was eventually arrived at: the Khan permitted that Herr Von Negri should sit in his presence. On the 20th December, at midday, we made our triumphal entry into Bokhara; in front of us rode a detachment of Cossacks, then came the presents destined for the Khan, which consisted of furs, porcelain, crystals, watches, and fire-arms; the remainder of the Cossacks, as well as the greater part of the infantry, brought up the rear. We were accompanied by a very distinguished Usbek, who could speak Persian fluently; he led us through a large gateway into the town of Bokhara, and going through a winding and narrow street, of which, on both sides, the houses were ridiculously small with flat roofs, we at last reached the college building, which formed the sides of a large open market-place, where we also perceived the doors of the Palace of the Khan. Having traversed open corridors, court-yards, and rooms, we at last reached the Hall of Audience, at one end of which, opposite the entrance door, the Khan sat; on his right stood the Koosh-beghi, and on his left his two sons, of whom the eldest seemed to be about 15 years of age.

On either side of the doorways stood five Noblemen; two chamberlains supported Herr Von Negri, who, approaching the Khan to within 10 paces, began to address him in Persian, and having handed over his credentials to the Koosh-beghi, he seated himself, whilst the remainder of the embassy went and ranged themselves against the walls on either side of the door.

The Koosh-beghi handed the letter of the Emperor to the Khan, who read it out loud; he then begged Herr Von Negri to allow a few Russian soldiers to enter the room, who were then told to put down their arms. The moment the Khan saw them, he began to laugh like a child; altogether his *tout ensemble* was wanting in expression: he was 45 years old; his beard was handsome, his eyes black, and his complexion of an olive-yellow. His physical energies appeared to have been completely dissipated in the harem: he wore a robe of black velvet adorned with jewels, and a muslin turban with a plume of heron's feathers: a golden scarf was placed diagonally across his turban, which thus resembled the Turkish "Kaleur," which is the gala head-dress of the Grand Vizirs, the Kapudan, Pashas, and Kizlar-agassis of the Porte.

The Koosh-beghi and three other gentlemen wore, instead of a turban, a conical cap of sable fur. The master of the ceremonies held in his

4

hand a sort of halberd, which at the top ended in an axe of solid silver: the presents were taken into another room within sight of the Khan. The audience lasted 20 minutes.

At its conclusion we once more found our escort outside the Palace, which was returning to Bazarschi, near which place they bivouaced for the whole of the remainder of the winter in a garden. Herr Von Negri, as well as the rest of the suite, was located in a large house in Bokhara belonging to the Koosh-beghi: we remained in this town from the 20th December 1820 until the 10th March 1821; we then proceeded to Bazarschi, and as the weather was fine, we preferred to biovouac in the garden of this little village: on the 22nd March we left Bazarschi, and on the 25th we bade farewell to Bokhara itself.

We were very glad to have seen the country, but we rejoiced still more as we left it behind us. The following notes regarding Bokhara itself as well as the neighbouring Khanates are partly derived from my own observations and partly acquired from other sources:—

CHAPTER VII.

The boundaries of Bokhara. Appearance of the country, climate, rivers,
towns, and villages.

As Bokhara is in itself a desert, and is also bounded by deserts, it is very difficult to fix its boundaries with any accuracy: the cultivated part of the country which lay on both sides of the road we came along only reaches to about 40 versts from Bokhara; still the boundary of the country itself extends much further to the north, and the Khan even sends his advanced posts as far as the sources of the Aghatma, where he has had a small house built for the convenience of the troops. The soldiers of his vassals are sometimes located still further beyond the Aghatma, where the Todjiks in the north-west collect wood and bring it into the market of Bokhara on camels' backs, and the Bokharian Customs Officers go as far as Kara-Ghata, where they inspect the caravans which come across from Russia: on the other hand, the Bokharians never pass Kara-Ghata unless they intend making a long journey; therefore, assuming an imaginary line drawn from this place to the frontier fortress of Ura-tepah, which is situated to the north-east of Samarcand, we may call this, to all intents and purposes, the northern boundary of Bokhara. The western boundary I thus define:—By drawing another line from Kara-Ghata, enclosing the wells of Tisch-Berdi; themselves lying on the road between Bokhara and Khiva, and in whose neighbourhood there is a Bokharian boundary village called Toitschi, which is situated on the banks of the Amoo. Mawri, in former days a well-known, but now a perfectly deserted town, is the place where the extreme Bokharian outpost on this side is placed.

The southern boundary of Bokhara is formed by another line, drawn from Mawri as far as the Amoo-Daria, which passes to the north of the Khanates Ankoi and Balkh, encloses Aghtschee, and extends as far as Deinan, which is the frontier town of the Khan of Hissar. The eastern boundary may be traced by a line drawn from Deinan to Ura-tepah, which encloses Fain, a town which is the most easterly of Bokhara.

The country of Bokhara lies between 41° and 37° North Latitude and between 61° and 66° 30′ East Longitude (Paris), and its area is about ten thousand geographical square miles.

The eastern part of the country is mountainous. The mountain chains run to the north of Bokhara, and terminate to the west of Samarcand in the neighbourhood of Karchi, and extend south to the Amoo-Daria. The whole of this western part consists of an undulating plain, studded with small hills, of the height of two or three toises, and varying in length and breadth from one or two to a hundred toises.

They are of clay, and similar to the ground of the deserts through which the Amoo River passes. The clay has a covering of loose sand, which now and then is raised in the form of hillocks, differing in shape and size; they are often perceived in the environs of Kizil-Kum.

In the whole of Bokhara there are only two rivers, which are very remarkable on account of their size and their usefulness to the agriculture of the country; they are the Zerafschan, also called the Kuwan, and the Kach-ka. The former flows from the far east of Samarcand, and passes within 12 versts to the north of Bokhara, where it divides and forms two arms. At this place it is about nine toises wide, and from three to four toises deep. The northern arm flows northwards until it loses itself in the fields of Waskend.

The Zerafschan, being the southern and nearer of the two to Bokhara, forms, about 40 versts from the Amoo, a lake called the Kara-Kul, which is about 50 versts in circumference, and whose waters are drained off in small canals, of which a few reach as far as Tschardjoui (Charjooee).

The Zerafschan and its canals irrigate the whole of the country lying between Mudjar to the east of Samarcand and Tschardjoui, especially the district of Miankal, which extends from Bokhara to Samarcand, and is the richest, the most productive, and the most populated part of the whole of Bokhara.

The most important of these canals, which is five toises in breadth, reaches to about 20 versts from Bokhara in a south-westerly direction. In the neighbourhood of Samarcand several small streams, as the Karabalik, i.e., black fish, join the Zerafschan.

Another small stream has its sources in the Muratagh, a high mountain about seventy versts from Bokhara; but in the summer time there is nothing left but a dry bed. The greater the amount of snow that falls on these mountains, the more this little stream swells out, and on its way to join the Waskend River contributes greatly to the productiveness of the soil about Bokhara itself. The fertility of the country being, therefore, to a great extent dependent on the amount of snow that falls on these hills, we can easily imagine this to be the origin of the custom of presenting a money prize to the person who brings the first news of the first fall of snow on this mountain. The Muratagh is the only mountain peak visible from the town of Bokhara, and the inhabitants have not been behindhand in making it the foundation of many an adventurous tale in which they have much faith. They tell one, for instance, with great gravity, that this mountain peak had been the spot where Noah's Ark had landed.

The water of this River Kach-ka is used to inundate the country round about the town of Karchi. This part is very fertile, and its products of rice, cotton, and fruits are brought for sale to Bokhara. This kind of irrigation absorbs the whole of the Kach-ka.

The Tupalak and the Zubrah, which flow into the Amoo, in the vicinity of Termez, are of little importance.

The oasis of Bokhara forms the loveliest and pleasantest sight imaginable; it is impossible to conceive a better cultivated land than these plains, covered with houses, gardens, and fields, the latter being in the shape of quadrangles and called Tanabs; their borders are about a foot in height, so as to keep in the water that is led to them. Thousands of small canals intersect this plain, on both banks of which, as well as on the sides of the mostly narrow roads, are rows of trees. The surface of the water in these canals is not all on the same level, so that at each junction there is a small cascade, the sound of which is agreeable to the ear. The trees, artificially planted in every direction, prevent the view from losing itself in the distance, and, besides making a pleasant impression, stand as a proof of the industry of the inhabitants.

The large number of dwelling-houses indicate a numerous population, too great to allow every member to be in perfectly easy circumstances.

The houses are mostly grouped together, thus forming villages, which are half hidden by the numerous fruit-trees. Several villages are completely surrounded by walls, sometimes perforated with embrasures, and even sometimes flanked by small towers, which, resembling small citadels, in great measure add to the picturesqueness of the country: these defences both prove the fear the inhabitants have of being attacked and plundered, and also remind the traveller of the frequent inroads and aggressions of the nomads in the Mavrennahar.

A Bokharian village generally contains about a hundred mud houses, which are separated from one another by as narrow streets as those of larger towns. In the centre one often sees a tank or well, which by means of a drain is kept constantly full.

Every one of these villages are close to some canal, so that the gardens can easily be watered. As a matter of course, the climate of the hilly districts of Bokhara must differ very much from that of the western part, which consists chiefly of an unbroken plain; and in future I shall refer only to the latter part. The different seasons are very regular. In the middle of February the fruit-trees begin to flower, and the other trees in the beginning of March.

Now begins the fine time of the year. The heavy rains, which last about three weeks, cease; the heat begins to become oppressive, and is the more perceptible on account of the atmosphere not being refreshed by storms. This season lasts until October, when there is a continuous downpour of rain for about two or three weeks. In November and December slight frosts, and sometimes even a little snow, act as harbingers to the coming winter, and yet I have myself seen melons in the fields on the 20th December, showing, therefore, that the cold could not have been severe.

The cold reaches its climax in January generally about 2° Reaumur, but sometimes it even reaches 8° Reaumur. The water is covered with ice about three or four inches thick, and occasionally the snow remains on the ground for about a fortnight at a time without any appearance of its thawing. The winter we spent in Bokhara was, according to the account of the inhabitants, unexceptionally mild. The water only froze for about four or five days, and the ice was only one inch in thickness, which the inhabitants broke up and collected in heaps covered with earth.

The rains begin again about the 7th or 15th February, and last till the end of the month; in a few days everything becomes green. Nothing can prove the extreme heat of the climate of Bokhara better than the power of the sun during the days of winter; in January we dined at midday in the open air; the thermometer in the shade showed 10° Reaumur, but in the sun it reached 22°. Strong winds are prevalent both in winter and summer, and lift to a great height the fine dust or sand which is everywhere met with, and which thus, as it were, hides everything from sight and darkens the atmosphere. These sand storms, which sometimes spread themselves over a whole district, can be seen 20 versts off. On the whole, the climate of Bokhara is healthy; the winter and the rainy seasons freshen and purify the atmosphere, and malarious vapours, which, issuing out of the ground, cause so many illnesses, are here unknown. The frequency of rheumatism is attributable to the dampness of the houses, and the numerous diseases of the eyes are caused by constant dust storms: total blindness is on this account common, so much so, that the father of the present Khan of Bokhara built a hospital for the blind, called the Fatah-bad, which is more like a monastery than anything else, and in which about 50 of the unfortunates live by twos and threes in small cells, which in themselves surround a mosque.

All the towns of Bokhara are situated on the banks of rivers, and are therefore surrounded by cultivated land. In the summer time the drought is sometimes so great that the inhabitants can only procure water by digging holes in the river bed; besides which, the plain of Bokhara itself lies very low, so that water can be found by digging down to 5, 7, or 8 feet. This stagnant water generates small worms, which are swallowed unconsciously, and this causes a well-known disease called by the Bokharians "Richta:" the whole body becomes covered with scabs, which become most painful abscesses: out of these come worms, which belong to the class of "Analides." As yet the Bokharians have not discovered a remedy for this; this same want of water once caused a Russian, who had been a prisoner in Bokhara, and with whom I was talking on this very subject, to exclaim that "heat was created by God in moments of wrath."

The towns of Bokhara which are south of the Amoo River are Kirkee, Aghtschee, Mawri, and Charjooee: in former days Mawri belonged to the Persians, and was then a flourishing city; it was taken by Morad Beg, the father of the present Khan of Bokhara: this was the glorious result of his frequent expeditions into Khorassan. His son, Emir Hayder, who most likely was afraid of the influence of his brother, Nassir Beg, at that time the owner of the town, ordered that all the inhabitants, about 25,000 in number, should be transported to the centre of Bokhara. Nassir Beg took flight to Mechehed in Persia, and Mawri became a wilderness. The Khan Emir Hayder keeps a garrison in Mawri of about 400 or 500 men, which are relieved triennially. Mawri is now-a-days looked upon as a place of banishment, to which those criminals are transported who have not received a capital sentence. This town once more contains about 500 inhabitants, and its environs are being restored; further, only a small number of canals are allowed to be led to this place from the Mubrab, which is about 20 versts distant, for the Khan will not permit Mawri to become a populated city, lest, on account of its isolated position, it should become independent.

Charjooee consists of about 1,000 houses, and, from fear of the inroads of the Khivans, also contains a tolerably strong garrison: the Khivans had attacked this town and plundered the inhabitants in the autumn of 1821. The towns which are in the neighbourhood of Bokhara are Kara-Kul, Khariabad, Buschenbeh, Tendani, Tscharschembeh, Ramitan, Zarimtan, Penschembeh-bazar, Wapken or Waskend, Urdenzei, and Ghudjbuan. Next to Bokhara, Parchie, and Samarcand, Kara-Kul is the largest town in Bokhara; it contains about 30,000 inhabitants. Urdenzei is a small fortress, which I visited on my way back to Russia, but we were forbidden to enter the town; most likely this order originated with higher authorities. It is called a fortress because it is surrounded by a mud wall about four toises in height: the cultivated districts extend to about five versts north of Urdenzei, and, on the desert which is beyond this cultivation, ruins of houses and traces of ancient canals were perceptible, proving that not very long since this portion of the country had also been cultivated. Its present barrenness as well as that near Kaghatan, which was buried by a sand storm about seven years ago, is attributable to the frequent winds blowing from the north-east, which for the last 10 years have been the curse of Bokhara; even during our journey we experienced the effects of this wind, and although it was disagreeable to do so, still I watched its dreadful ravages with the greatest interest.

On the 25th March 1821 we left Urdenzei: the wind was tolerably strong, though not tempestuous: we had hardly left the argillaceous tract, and had entered upon the small sand hills previously alluded to, when the wind began to increase in force; whirlwinds of sand rose into the air and penetrated everything; to protect my eyes, I had had made a sort of spectacles which turned out of no use; the sand rose in the form of a cloud into the air, darkened the sun so that one could only see for a very short distance ahead, and Kirghizzee guides could no longer discover the route. As luck would have it, a cavalry soldier of the Bokharian garrison had followed us as far as Urdenzei to see if any Russian slaves had mixed themselves up with our escort; we compelled him by placing a pistol at his ear to become our guide: although the service was very much against his wishes, still it prevented us from losing our road. One can hardly imagine anything more disagreeable than this sand, for although it is large-grained, it still penetrates the eyes, ears, and mouth; the eyes of all our party became inflamed, and I can quite understand how it was the army of Nadir Shah, at the time of crossing the desert, to the west of the Amoo, during one of these storms, lost so many men by ophthalmia. On this account one may look upon the deserts which surround Bokhara as a natural defence to the country; the sand-drifts caused by the storms alluded to, fill up the ditches and accumulate alongside the walls of the towns, and, reaching a great height, sometimes completely fill up the streets and cover the houses, like the ashes of Vesuvius, which burned Herculaneum and Pompei. In the neighbourhood of Urdenzei the sand encroaches yearly on the cultivated land, and whatever pains the inhabitants take to clear the sand from their ditches, they are unsuccessful as a rule; and it is most probable that, at some future time, the fertile and smiling oases of Bokhara will become barren and deserted, just as those of Sedjistan, whose former fertility is commemorated by splendid ruins, which are still visible, although Sedjistan itself is nothing more than sand and pebbles.

The remaining towns of Bokhara are little worthy of mention; they contain about 500 houses, besides a market-place in which now and then fairs are held. The town of Waskend, which I visited, contains about 300 houses, built in a most irregular manner, but the minaret of the mosque is still very handsome. The only difference between the towns and the villages consists generally in difference of administration and in the relative importance of the fairs held in them, at which most of the merchants of Bokhara buy up their wares for export. In the district of Miankal we find Kermineh, Penschembeh, Ziawudin, Katirschi, Katto-Kinghan, Zenghi-Kinghan, Karchi, Gheldhi-Kinghan, and Tschalak. All these towns are situated in a fertile part of the country, and are of a very fair size, and the rich amongst the Usbeks own houses in them, where they come to spend the summer in order to be near their herds.

To the south of Uuratagh are Niwatazee, Metan, Drourtaoul, Jarbaschi, and Kara-Kazam. Samarcand forms a part of Bokhara since its conquest by the Khan Abullah of Kermineh, who has made himself remarkable by the number of edifices which he has built: his reign lasted from 1564 to 1592.

The Khan of Bokhara travels once a year to Samarcand; at his elevation to the Khanate he has to go to Samarcand and to sit on the "Kuktach," a rectangular stone of blue marble about $1\frac{1}{2}$ toises in height, which is placed in the Maddrassu of Mirza Olug Beg: he is enclosed in a white blanket, in which he is lifted up and down three times in the air; its four corners are held by the Ulemas (Mollahs), the Fakivahs, the Miankals, and Sayuds. It is supposed that a throne should be made out of this stone, which was brought from the Ghaghan Mountain. Samarcand contains about 50,000 inhabitants: its musjids and maddrassus (Colleges) are finer buildings than those of Bokhara; they are built of white marble, the quarries of which exist at a short distance from the old capital of the Timurs. The tombs of these Timurs are still to be seen in Samarcand; they are made of jasper, but one seeks in vain for the traces of the observatoria of Olug Beg. The civilization of the Timurs had to give way to the barbarous Usbeks.

To the north of Samarcand we find the forts Ura-tepah, Lamur, and Djisagh, which always contain large garrisons, also the town Djain, Kara-tepeh, and Zenghi-Kinghan.

Fani is a small town to the east of Samarcand close to the sources of Zerafschan, which does not, as is stated by geographers, form a lake as far as Kara-Kul.

Falgah, Margian, and Kastut are situated along the banks of this river. Urghut, Pendja-Kent, Wrimtan, Kara-tepeh, Katilas, are to the south of Samarcand. I must be satisfied with mentioning the names only of these places, for their localities I have learnt from hearsay. Karchi or Nakhchev is on account of its size an important town; it is situated on the main road, and some of the caravans which come from Herat or Cabul make a halt here, or diverge at this point towards Samarcand without passing through Bokhara.

Karchi is also employed as a depôt for the furs of martins, foxes, and unborn lambs, which come from the south of Bokhara, and are then sold in the capital. The exports of Karchi are dried fruits, raw and spun cotton, tobacco, and a little silk; this town generally contains a garrison of from 2,000 to 3,000 men. To the east of Karchi we find Tscharagatschi and Ghussar, both important towns. In the neighbourhood of the former the Khan possesses considerable property, and round about the latter there are nothing but half-nomad Usbeks; for this reason the appointment of a Governor of Ghussar is one of the most important in the whole of the Khanate: this was held by Emid Hayder. During the life-time of his father, Tauraka, the eldest son of the present Khan, was Hakim of Kinnineh, a town mostly inhabited by Usbeks, who were also in large numbers in the neighbourhood; but having quarrelled with his father, he was recalled. Of Termez, on the Amoo, the sole remains are ruins.

This town is situated on the left bank of the Amoo, and exactly opposite to Cheimed; altogether everything goes to prove that the district of Saghdiana or the Mavrennahar had formerly been more wealthy than Bokhara is at present. To sum up the list of the towns of Bokhara I need only mention Bosin and Chirabad; they both lie to the north of Temir.

An inhabitant of Bokhara assured me that the old town, Ostruch, was situated half way on the road between Balkh and Chehri-sebz, and not anywhere near where the Arab geographers place the country of Osruchna. Nobody could give me any information regarding a cave near this tower out of which during the night a flaming vapour is said to appear. But inasmuch as Farganah has changed its name, too, it is very probable that Osruchna is no longer known by that name.

CHAPTER VIII.

The Capital: its houses; streets; remarkable buildings; inhabitants.

I HAVE been told that the name Bokhara was first used by an Arab historian of the tenth century, who, writing about a certain country in the Mavrennahar of the name of Bokharia, mentions that it had been conquered by the Arabs in the year 684, but that its capital was not captured till the year 699.

Between the years 896 and 998 Bokhara was governed by the Samanide dynasty, which continued in a flourishing state.

Being conveniently situated for the purpose of commerce, it rapidly became wealthy, but, in so doing, excited the rapacity of the barbarians, who plundered it. It was then burnt to the ground by the hordes of Jhingis Khan, who did not have it rebuilt till near his end.

In the days of Timur it was restored, and once more flourished, although this conqueror preferred Samarcand, where he generally resided. After the Timurs had ceased to reign in Samarcand, Bokhara was chosen by the Khans of the Usbeks as their place of residence, and a few of them had even erected mosques and maddrassus, although they completely quenched the love for arts and science and destroyed the traces of a civilization which was opposed to the character of these nomad people. It is well known how fond the Orientals are of sprinkling their history with dashes of the fabulous; it is therefore quite in accordance with their feeling that they should have a tale as to the origin of their capital, which in itself is far from being improbable.

Accordingly, it is said that in former ages the country round about Bokhara was covered with lakes, which, on account of their abundance of fish, had attracted numbers of fishermen, who having prospered had taken to agriculture. The population increased gradually more and more, till at last houses took the places of cabins, and in course of time a town was built. This became Bokhara. In after-years it became celebrated in the East on account of its schools and learned Mollas; and because some holy men were buried within its walls, it became a place of pilgrimage for all Mahomedans. This may also be the reason why it received the soubriquet of Elcherifah, *i.e.*, the holy or the noble.

In some oriental book or other I saw it mentioned that in the Mongolian language "buh" meant "to study" or "the studies," "knowledge," and "ara" "treasure," so that Bokhara would mean "treasure of studies," or the "treasury of studies."

Abul Ghazi in his works makes some remarks which coincide with this conclusion; he says that "Bokhara" means a "learned man," and also that all who wished to study languages or sciences used to go to Bokhara.*

* The following is an extract from a book on geography by Heidgee Khalfa (p. 351) in the Turkish translation printed in Constantinople:—

"Buchara is a renowned city situated 97°50' by 39°50' latitude, and Habil-ul sair (friend of truth), derives it from the word "Buchar," which, in the language of the unbelievers, means "the place of gathering of science."

Several writers, with whose opinions some of our own geographers agree, state that the capital town of Mavrennahar must have been called Bikend, and that its ruins are seen up to the present time in the neighbourhood of Zerafschan in the direction of Cabul, and about 30 versts distant from Bokhara, planted with avenues of trees and numerous gardens, so that one cannot see to a long distance for this reason. Bokhara first comes to view only at a distance of three versts, when approaching it from Waskend. The first view of the capital is startling in effect to a European. Domes, mosques, the points of the castellated roofs of the colleges, the minarets, the palaces, which spring out of the centre of the town, a lake close to the walls, surrounded by flat-roofed houses, or prettily decorated summer-houses, and, lastly, fields, gardens, trees, and the life and movement which is always observable in a capital city,—all these tend to make a favourable impression. But the delusion soon dissipates on approaching the town, for, with the exception of the public baths, mosques, and colleges, one sees only dirty, grey-coloured mud-houses, built here and there, without any notion of order, thereby making the streets dirty, crooked, and winding.

These houses, which are fronted towards the court-yards, appear towards the street as nothing more or less than bare walls without windows and without anything that could gratify the eye of the passenger. On the contrary, everything that is to be seen in this populous capital seems to hint at mistrust, and hardly ever do the faces of the inhabitants express any signs of joy. Such things as noisy festivities are here unknown, nor does one ever hear music and singing, and nothing tends to show that the people occasionally indulge in pleasure, or that they enjoy their existence. On this account, when we entered the town, our feeelings of curiosity and interest, which had been at first excited on perceiving the oriental style in which it was built, soon gave way to those of sadness and depression. The finest streets in Bokhara are not much more than one toise broad, and the smaller ones being mostly only three or four feet wide are only practicable for foot passengers. Even in the broadest streets one runs a risk of being knocked about, and hurt by the brushwood with which the camels are laden, and which occupies a good deal of space. Besides which the streets are generally crowded by men, horses, camels, and donkeys, and if one wishes to ride through this crowd, one must constantly call out "poch," "poch." This multitude of horses and camels makes very deep footprints in the streets, which add to their filth and discomfort, which is very evident when one passes through them. The wall surrounding Bokhara, which is similar to those of Persian towns, is four toises in height, and its thickness at the base is the same. It is divided into three parts, which gradually decrease in size towards the top, which is only four feet wide. At small intervals it is flanked by round towers; in some parts it projects in such a manner as to convey the idea that it had been originally intended to construct bastions; but considering that one side alone is about two versts in length, it seems that these projections are only the result of accident. Bokhara has 11 gates, the Tniam, Samarcand, Manasai, Karchi, Schahan, Nemaz Ghiah, Chadjelal, Kara-Kul, Chirgharam, Tol-palak, and Oghlam; they are all built of brick, and flanked by two round towers; they are generally guarded by a file of men, and they are opened and closed at sunrise and sunset respectively. I one day rode round the town of Bokhara, and found it to be about 14 versts in circumference; it contains 8,000 houses and nearly 70,000 inhabitants: three-fourths of the number are Tadjiks, artizans and laborers; the remainder consist of Usbeks, Jews, Tartars, Affghans, Kalmucks, Hindoos, of merchants belonging to the neighbouring Khanates, a few pilgrims, Persian and Russian slaves, and of a small number of Negroes and Scia-pouches.

The Jews own in Bokhara about 800 houses; according to their own account, having left Bagdad 700 years, they came across from Samarcand.

Of all the towns of Central Asia, Bokhara contains the greatest number of Jews, and may be looked upon as their principal residence in the East. Mechehed contains 300 Jewish houses, Cheriseds and Balkh about 30 each, Samarcand and Herat only 10, and Khiva 4: Badakshan,

Kokan, and Kashgar have no Jewish inhabitants at all. The Jews of Bokhara have very well-shaped heads, a pale complexion, and large fiery and expressive eyes.

The Jews in Bokhara are only permitted to live in three streets, and although, as they state themselves, they are treated better here than in any other town in Central Asia, still they are despised and oppressed in several ways by the Government itself.

For instance, every Jewish landlord has to pay a monthly tax of four tongas, or three rubles, in the shape of a draft on a Bank. After their sixteenth year every Jew of moderate wealth has to pay two tongas per mensem; a poorer one, only half.

This poll tax brings in about eighty thousand rubles per annum. Only two capitalist Jews are known; the remainder being fairly well off occupy themselves by commerce in raw and spun silks, dyeing, and manufacture. They are prohibited from riding through the town, from wearing silk, and their caps are only allowed to have a border of two inches in width. They are forbidden to build a new synagogue, but can restore the old one. These degrading customs are precisely the same that Jews and Christians are subject to in the whole Osman Empire.

The Rabbi of Bokhara, who was born in Algiers, and could still talk a little Spanish, told me that on his first arrival in the place he found the Jews perfectly ignorant; only a few of them could write, and they only had two copies of their holy writ, a book containing only the first three books of the Pentateuch and nothing more. This Algierian Jew, an intelligent old man, who had nearly burst into tears on once more seeing the faces of Europeans, has in no wise neglected to educate and better his brethren. He has founded a school, has sent for books from Russia, Bagdad, and Constantinople, so that now there is not a Jew who cannot read and write. They study the "Talmud," although they deviate from its instructions in several things.*

The Tartars in Bokhara have been estimated about three thousand, and are all Russian subjects. They consist mostly of run-away criminals and soldiers. The remainder have come here to try their luck, and about three hundred of them study religion.

Since 1817 the number of Affghans has very much increased owing to the quantity of emigrants from Cabul, who, on account of the disturbances in their own country, have sought refuge here: at present they already number about two thousand. A couple of hundred of Kalmucks also inhabit Bokhara, few of them owning land in the neighbourhood of the town, but the greater part of them are soldiers. Within the last four or five years the number of Hindoos has been much augmented, and about three hundred of them have settled down as merchants; they have mostly come from Cabul and Mooltan, but a few also from Shikarpoor. They have an orange-red-coloured mark on their foreheads, which, according to their caste, is either vertical or horizontal.

The merchants that visit Bokhara consist of those of all countries who deal with this town, but are mostly Russians (excepting Tartars), Khokans, also from Task-kend and Persia, but none from China or Thibet.

---

* For instance, they do not cut the bride's hair, nor do they cover her head with a cloth during the wedding ceremonies, &c.

A few from Cashmere also live here; they are remarkable for their beauty of figure: one especially took my fancy; he was tall, with splendid black eyes, an aquiline nose, and a large beard. I told him that I would have taken him for a handsome Jew, but he did not seem to like this simile, as I might have known before. But, on the other hand, this similarity was so striking, that seeing this man one would feel very much inclined to agree with those who believe Cashmere to be a Jewish colony.

In the caravanserais of Bokhara I have seen several Affghans from the eastern mountains; they have fine and expressive, but wild-looking, features. On addressing them they answered in such a gruff voice that it seemed as if they were cursing and swearing. These Affghans, as well as the Kirghizzees, do not care much for the Police regulations of Bokhara; they dress differently to the Affghans from Cabul, for they only have one long linen sheet wrapped round them, like the togas of the Roman Senators. Although Mahomedans, and, like the Bokharians, belonging to the Sunnite sect, still they shave nothing, but the very top of their heads, thus letting their hair fall down over their ears and neck: this is why they are called "kafirs," or "unbelievers," by the inhabitants of Bokhara. Most of the pilgrims that come to Bokhara are beggars, who, like the Schamaric sorcerers, earn their daily bread by exhibiting their bodily ailments. They affect being insane, for the people of this country look upon all those who are mentally deranged with a sort of holy awe.

Every wealthy and respectable inhabitant of Bokhara owns slaves, mostly Persians; the number of Russian slaves is only ten at present, for the others have bought their liberty: but as "kafirs" are still despised, those who have gone over to the Mahomedan religion are always looked upon with suspicion. Taking them altogether, the number of slaves in Bokhara comes up to several thousands.

The most remarkable building in this town is the Khan's Palace, which by the inhabitants is called "Arck," and is said to have been built by Arslan Khan quite ten centuries ago. It is situated on an eminence and surrounded by a wall ten toises in height. The gateway is of brick and flanked on both sides by towers fifteen toises high.

A large "corridor" or passage, the vaults of which seem to be very old, lead to the top of the eminence, where are the earth-built houses inhabited by the Khan himself and his Court. Here are to be seen a mosque, the house of the Khan and that of his children, the harem, which, surrounded by gardens, is completely hidden amongst the trees, a house in which the Koosh-beghi works and gives audience, another in which he lives himself (which here is considered a great favour), and lastly, the apartments for the body guard, the slaves, the stable, &c., &c.

Some storks have built their nests in the highest works of the two gate towers, making a curious impression on the European traveller. Their position seems certainly derogatory to a Court belonging to a Sovereign of the "Glorious East."

After evening prayer the sentries in the Palace are doubled and the large gate closed; this is also the case with all the city gates.

The minaret or tower of Mirgbaral, which stands close to the main mosque "Musjid-kalan," and according to some has been erected by Timur, according to others by Kizil-Arslan Khan, seems to me to be the best example of the style of architecture in vogue here. It is thirty toises high, and at its base has a circumference of about twelve toises. Its proportions are good and elegant; the bricks of which it is built are laid in with taste, and the tower itself, although of such antiquity, is in a very good condition.

Bokhara contains 360 mosques, and curiously enough, there is always one either close or opposite one of the schools. These mosques show a greater variety of architecture than the college buildings; besides this, nearly all the larger buildings, on account of their vaulted shapes, indicate traces of that style chiefly used by the Moors.

The largest mosque is that which one sees in the market-place called Sedjistan and opposite to the Palace; its front is the most elaborately decorated of all: slates of various colours are let in in such a way as to represent bouquets of flowers, and in some places even difficult texts out of the Koran. The ground colour of this slate is blue; the decorations white.

The colleges, which are very similar to one another, are in the forms of parallelograms, and are two stories high. The prettiest and best decorated with these variegated slates is the one built by Subban Cooli Khan, who died in Bokhara in 1702; but the largest is the one of Kolkatach, which properly contains three, of which one college is called El-Nassir Etshi: this school owns its existence to the generosity of the Russian Empress Catherine II., who sent 40,000 Rubles to Bokhara for its erection; her name is always spoken of by the inhabitants with the greatest respect and admiration. The arches of the entrances to these colleges are often split, which is caused by frequent earthquakes, to which the country is subject.

Bokhara contains the following fourteen caravanserais :—

1st, that of Abdulla Jan; 2nd, that of the Koosh-beghi; 3rd, that of the Hindoos; 4th, Nogais; 5th, that of Khodja Jonibar; 6th, that of Task-kend; 7th, of Karchi; 8th, of Miragul; 9th, of the Emirs; 10th, that of Kullata; 11th, of Fichana; 12th, of Danculla Chir; 13th and 14th, those of Urghenj: these last two are the smallest of all, and the Abdulla Jan Serai, built A.D. 1819, is the largest; they are all laid out on the same plan, namely, a quadrilateral of buildings enclosing a large court-yard.

On all sides are rooms or booths generally two stories high; the hire of one of these rooms is about 14 francs per month, and although they are very small, still they have to be both shop and dwelling-room.

As most of the caravanserais have been built by subscription, the income derived from them is given to the colleges and Mollas of the mosque attached.

In Bokhara I came across a Tartar merchant who had hired one of these stalls in a caravanserai for his store, and another, which he found drier and warmer than the former, as a room to live in. I remarked to him that it must be very disagreeable to live in such a place when any idle man can go in and out of every room to try to kill time by entering into conversation with its inmates; this is an inconvenience to which every lodger in a caravanserai must subject himself to, as custom forbids anybody locking his door and shutting himself up.

The large number of shops and booths proves that Bokhara is a populous town, carrying on an extensive trade.   Besides the shops in the caravanserais, there are large arched buildings with several entrances, containing hundreds of stalls, filled mostly with the silk productions of the country.   There are sheds half a verst in length, both sides of which are nothing but shops, &c.: an entire one of these shop-rows contains nothing but young women's slippers; another one, all kinds of raw-materials and aromatic substances, which fill the atmosphere with an agreeable perfume; a third, ornaments and precious stones, mostly of small value, such as, for instance, Parian, Turkish, and Tartar rubies, which come from the Badakshan Lake in Arabia, golden head-pieces (tiaras), studded with inferior turquoises for the Tartar women, &c., &c. Other large vaulted buildings are filled with dried fruits and tobacco, others with pistachios, with manna or with fresh and dried plums, grapes, pomegranates, and melons, which are hung up in bunches on the walls; amongst the shops are also the "refreshment" booths, where are to be had pilaos of various descriptions.

One can also see tents of all colours, which are mostly pitched in the Sedjistan, or large market-place, the remaining space of which is used for the selling of wood, vegetables, rice, wheat, and jugera, as well as of all kinds of fruits, bread, and other necessaries of life, required by a numerous population.

The Sedjistan being such a frequented place, all executions take place in it: here the criminals are hanged, and the heads of the enemy fallen in battle are either stuck upon poles, or placed on the ground, close to the gallows.   The people are so accustomed to these sights, that they take no notice of them and quietly continue their business.

In the other market-places are sold cotton stuffs, coloured linens, hay, &c., and everything that is necessary for the stable, or for the keeping of horses.   Lastly, in some of the road-crossings, which are vaulted and supported by thick columns, are silks, ribbons, knives, lighting materials, bad tea, horse-cloths, &c.

Bokhara contains sixty-eight wells; they are mostly small water-tanks, about one hundred and twenty feet in circumference: the water in them is stagnant, but is removed by means of canals that extend all over the city.   Of public bathing-places, all of them spacious, there are fourteen.

Moreover, everything in Bokhara tends to show that it must at one time have been in a far greater and more flourishing state than it is now-a-days.

A greater part of the mosques and colleges are crumbling to pieces, and they are all in bad repair.   I observed the same regarding the stone stairs that lead into the wells, which are never renewed.   The art of making the blue tiles, with which all public buildings are de-corated, has been forgotten, and the state of even the private houses shows that, in former times, Bokhara itself was governed better than it is at present.

CHAPTER IX.

The inhabitants of Bokhara, Usbeks, Tadjiks, Turcomans, Arabs, Kalmucks,
Kirghizzees, Kara-Kalpaks, Afghans, Lesghees, Jews, Gipsies.

The inhabitants of Bokhara may be divided into two principal
classes, namely, the conquerors and the conquered. The Usbeks are
the former, the Tadjiks the latter, who look upon themselves as the
aborigines, and probably are descended from the Sogdians; they generally
are of small stature, with European features, black hair, and a good
complexion, which is much fairer than that of the Persians.

The Usbeks, who claim the land round about Astrachan as their original
country, are divided into a great many tribes, of which the most
respectable is that of the Manghuts, to which the Khan also belongs.
This tribe is in itself divided into the Kara-Manghuts, the Fok-Manghuts,
and the Ak-Manghuts. The principal of the remaining tribes are Jahu,
Kalluk, Kalmuck, Naiman, Khitai, Kipt-Shak, Kirk, Jai, and Uring.

Besides these two classes, there are also Turcomans, Arabs, Kalmucks, Kirghizzees, Kara-Kalpaks, Afghans, Lyhees (Lesghees), Jews,
Gipsies, and several thousands of slaves, mostly Persians. It would,
indeed, be hard to find another country the population of which would
consist of as many different kinds of people as there are in Bokhara.
The features of the Usbeks show that they have a little Tartar and Kalmuck blood in them. They have principally settled down in the
neighbourhood of Samarcand, Bokhara, Kara-Kul, Karchi, Ghussar, and
Miankal.

The Turcomans, who have a wider face and a smaller figure
than the Usbeks, are still more like the Kalmucks. Their strongest
tribe is that of Teki: they are nomads, and live on the left bank of
the Amoo-Daria from Kirkee as far as the borders of Khiva. They do
not like going beyond Jouchi on the right bank, as there, on account
of the sandy plains, they cannot find any pasturage.

As irrigation is convenient all along the banks of the Amoo,
the Turcomans cultivate rice in great quantities. They also possess
fields not far from Mawri, which they consider too few already, so
that it seems as if the population was increasing. They are not so
wealthy as the Kirghizzees, and have no numerous herds; their largest
contains about sixty horses, which by-the-by are dearer amongst them
than with the Kirghizzees. The Chiefs of the Turcomans have the title
of Beg; they pay the tributes, called Ghochour and Zekiat, to the
Khan of Bokhara, who would treat them as enemies did they not
pay these as the sign of the supremacy of the Prince over their hordes.
Inasmuch as Russia has extended her protection to the large and
middle horde of the Kirghizzees, and has protected it from the attacks
of the enemy, she is also entitled to levy these tributes, which are
prescribed by the Koran. Arabs have settled down in Bokhara
ever since the time when this land was conquered by the Kalifs;
one recognizes them at first sight by their dark-brown complexion:
they live in villages, a few of which are in the neighbourhood of Bokhara.

A few Arabs wander about as nomads, others as half-nomads, in the neighbourhood of Karchi and Termez. A good many amongst them are cultivators, and possess herds of cattle, which are taken to graze in the steppes, and these are the principal people that deal in the well-known unborn lambskins.

The greater part of the Kalmucks in Bokhara are descended from the hordes of Jhingis Khan; the remainder belong to the so-called Forgut Kalmucks, who, in the year 1770, left the banks of the Volga to settle down in Bokhara: the former have nearly completely forgotten their mother-tongue, and amongst themselves speak the Tartar language. One can only recognize them by their features; they are celebrated for their courage, and have adopted all the ways and usages of the Usbeks, amongst whom they live in their own villages in the districts Miankal and others.

The Kirghizzees of Bokhara are mostly runaways or deserters from the smaller hordes, who have wandered to new steppes there to try their fortune. Being such vagabonds they think nothing of undertaking long and tedious journeys; they thus sometimes leave Bokhara and return to their steppes, which they often again relinquish. They are to be found in the north-east of Bokhara in the neighbourhood of Karchi, and also to the north of Miankal, where they meet the Kara-Kalpaks, who treat them as compatriots. Some of the Afghans and the Lesghees of Bokhara are descended from the hostages taken by Timur. A similar origin is ascribed to the Kitais (Chinese). The Sesghees are only a few in number; they live in the neighbourhood of Samarcand, and still speak their own language.

The Gipsies, who are called in Bokhara Maganes, are of unknown origin, and they are to be met with in every part of the country; as everywhere else they occupy themselves in fortune-telling and horse-dealing. Travelling about in small bands, they spend their miserable lives in tents, and their women, who go about unveiled, manage, as formerly, since the Bokharian Police is not very strict, to make a good trade with their charms.

The character of the Bokharian is cringing and deceitful, as is the case with all Orientals who languish under the yoke of despotism. The features of a Tadjik have always the expression of good nature and of perfect tranquillity; thus he appears to be a mild, good, and obliging individual, although he is by nature a false, blackguardly, deceitful, and avaricious one. Thirst for money destroys all feelings of humanity, and, next to the Arabs, the Tadjiks are the most cruel masters towards their slaves; in other respects they are diligent and energetic, and understand their business: they are merchants, artizans, and cultivators. The life of a nomad has no charm for them, though the greater part can read and write, and, with the exception of the clergy, they form the most civilized class of the population of Bokhara: but, they are arrant cowards, and ever since they have inhabited Bokhara, they have played a subordinate part. Never has one of them dared to seize the Government.

The Tadjiks have never been known to take up arms, and have never defended their country; on the other hand, the Usbek is a warrior heart and soul, and his military ardour is kept alive by constant feuds with his neighbours. Even the most insignificant of the Usbeks feel that they belong to the race of conquerers and masters of the land, and in every one of them are still to be discovered the traces of that pride which is peculiar to the Turkish races, which often borders on arrogance, but which nevertheless retains the germ of greatness. Their national pride shows itself particularly when any one asks them if they are Usbeks: the "yes," which comes out with particular significance, is very expressive. I have often heard Usbeks bitterly complain that the Khan did not allow them to revenge their compatriots for the attacks and robberies made by the Khivans. "We have," they say, "to feel ashamed before you strangers for allowing ourselves to be so insulted; we are warriors; we are courageous; we possess excellent horses, and if the Khan would only give us permission, we would revenge ourselves on the Khivans by conquering them, killing or taking them prisoners, as we did 10 years ago."

Their courage, as is the case with the Turks, partakes more of the character of foolhardiness, and the calmness, the *sang-froid*, and the steadiness of European soldiers, who fight for the love of their country and who are led by the feelings of duty, are unknown to them. However different the Usbeks are with regard to courage from the Tajiks, still, these two races are very much alike in other respects, especially in their avarice and selfishness. Many of the Usbeks trade, particularly those who hold appointments under Government; the consequence is, that avariciousness and the thirst for gain cause a good deal of bribery and injustice. The spirit of tale-bearing, intrigue, and jealousy which is so common in an Oriental Court has a very bad influence on the character of the Khan's favourites, who are well up in the art of deceiving and of cringing on suitable occasions. In a land where cunning is considered a talent, deceit regarded as a duty, and imposition looked upon as a virtue, there can be of course little attention paid to good-faith, and the blessings of open-heartedness and trust are unknown. With regard to population, it is very difficult to estimate the number in a country which contains so many different races, some of whom lead a nomad life, and a census has never been attempted. In order to ascertain the facts as accurately as possible, we have made enquiries from all the people in Bokhara who could give us any reliable information.

The cultivated portion of this Khanate may be estimated at 300 square German miles, or 12,000 square hours. Supposing that one allowed 5,000 inhabitants to the square mile (as in the richest part of Italy), we should have as a result $1\frac{1}{2}$ million of inhabitants who live by cultivation, or half as nomads, or in the towns; to this must be added about 1 million of nomads, so that the whole of the population of Bokhara may be estimated at $2\frac{1}{2}$ millions, subdivided as follows :—

				Population.
Usbeks	...	...	...	1,500,000
Tajiks	...	...	...	650,000
Turcomans	...	...	...	200,000
Arabs	...	...	...	50,000
Persians	...	...	...	40,000
Kalmucks	...	...	...	20,000
Kirghizzees and Kara-Kalpuks			...	60,000
Jews ...	...	...	...	4,000
Afghans	...	...	...	4,000
Lesghees	...	...	...	2,000
Gipsies	...	...	...	2,000
		Sum total	...	2,532,000

CHAPTER X.

Cultivation, Industry, and Commerce.

Cultivation is the chief source of the national wealth : a profusion and variety of products not only meet the wants of the population itself, but suffice for a large trade. This means of livelihood could, in this country, be much augmented if it was not contrary to the character and mode of living of the greater portion of the inhabitants to better themselves ; besides which, one great drawback to cultivation is the want of water, which is so essential to the soil and climate of this country. A proper method of dividing the fields could in a great measure obviate this difficulty, but, alas ! how can one expect perfection so long as the land is steeped in darkness, and so long as its inhabitants adhere to the ancient practice of slavery, which is opposed to the first principles of progress. The cultivation of the soil, which is left to the slaves, brings in a larger income in Bokhara than anywhere else ; the reason for this is the uncommonly productive character of the country and the small extent of the estates, which, as a rule, are divided into many parts, thus enabling the masters better to supervise. Land properties are of five different kinds : 1st, the possession of the Government (crown lands), which, of course, are the largest ; 2nd, "Karadjis," or those possessions which formerly were disputed with the Government by individuals, but which have now been ceded to the latter for a small sum of money ; 3rd, life properties given as rewards for military service ; 4th, "Milks," or private landed estates ; 5th, "Wakfs," or religious endowments.

The crown lands, as well as many other estates, are rented : the Government claims two-fifths of the produce. The irrigation canals, on which depends the fertility of the soil, run down from the rivers, and where this can't take place, the land remains uncultivated : these canals, which are constructed with great care, and laid out according to correct calculations of level, with regard to the quantity of water required, &c., and are, therefore, of different breadths and depths, are very easily filled up by sand and clay ; when this occurs, they are then, as in Egypt, cleaned under the superintendence of a "Merab," who is appointed by Government, and who has the entire management of irrigation, whence arises a great deal of oppression and injustice. The soil is also manured, but on account of the scarcity of the pasturage and the dearness of the hay, there is very little cattle to be met with on these estates, so that manure is scarce ; besides which, the inhabitants of Bokhara use it as fuel. In some parts the ground is so saturated with salt, that its surface presents a crust of salt, and, before it can be used, it has to be mixed with other soil. Wood and iron are here very dear ; the agricultural implements are of a lasting character, and are well made. The plough is generally drawn by bullocks : the carts which are used for transporting soil or for bringing in the crops have only two large and clumsy wheels, and are so far useful, that they are not easily upset in crossing small drains. The merchants of Kokan use similar vehicles for the conveyance of their goods ; one can, therefore, conclude that the passes of the mountains between Samarcand and Kojend cannot be very difficult.

The fields are divided into Tanahs of an area of 3,000 square yards; the value of the fields varies with the quality of the soil, convenience of situation with regard to water supply, and distance from market-places and towns: it lies between 200 and 2,000 paper rubles. The average value of a Tanah is about 600 rubles. In the autumn they sow wheat, and reap it in July; immediately afterwards the fields are again ploughed up, and beans or peas are sown, which are also gathered within the year. Besides the common pea, they have another kind, which is darker and smaller in size than linseed; this is called " Mach:" this pea is the principal source of nourishment used by the poor, and it is very cheap. When an Usbek wishes to chaff a poor Tajik, he calls him by the name of mackfresser (pea-guzzler); he, in return, calls the nomad Usbek knit-fresser (cheese-guzzler, who has not even bread). With the Mach, Kundjit, and Taghar are sown two kinds of sesame, from the gum of which oil is extracted.

The Bokharians also cultivate beans called Lubia. Barley is sown the first week in March, and is gathered in before the wheat; it takes the place of oats, which are scarce in Bokhara: the Djugera *(Holcus saccharatus)* is sown in the middle of March, and gathered in before the end of July; its seed is white, and of the size of small peas; it is given to horses. It fattens readily, but is not as strengthening as oats or barley. Djugera is also used to make flour, which the poor mix up with wheat flour in making bread. Its stalk is about five feet high and about an inch in diameter; at its root it has leaves one foot in length, and is often sown a second time, at the end of the summer, for the purpose of growing green food for cattle; it requires a moist soil and warm weather; besides, the stalks have to be a foot apart: moreover, it belongs to the class of products such as wheat and melons, which extract the most virtue from the soil.

Rice is unknown in the neighbourhood of Bokhara, but in the Mian-kal it is produced in large quantities, though of a bad description; a great deal of it is brought from the Chebrisebs, and even from India, this latter being the most sought after. As there is no pasturage in the oasis of Bokhara, a kind of grass is sown in the Tanahs, which grows uncommonly quick, and is cut four or five times in the year; this kind of grass, which is sold instead of hay, is very nourishing, and is to be had fresh all the year round. Manna is found in great quantities in Bokhara, and is used in making various dishes and comfits; it is found in the mornings lying like dew on a plant called the " Tikan," which is very common in the deserts of Karchi: to collect the manna a blanket or sheet is placed underneath this plant, which is then shaken. In Bokhara it goes by the name of " Terendjebin," and the syrup, which is extracted from it, is called " Rustee," and costs about seven sous the pound.

We came across several of the common kitchen plants of Europe, as, for instance, cabbages, beet-roots of different kinds (which by-the-by were never preserved), cucumbers, onions, and excellent melons, with a green rind and white inside. Potatoes and artichokes are, however, unknown in Bokhara. The western part of this country is quite open and without any trees; all wood used here for building, &c., is fetched from the mountains of Samarcand, from whence it is floated down the River Zerafschau as far as Bokhara and Kara-Kul. The trees one sees in the oasis are either sown or planted, and shoot up in no time; they generally are either willows, poplars, plantain trees, or fruit and mulberry trees: besides these, there is one remarkably pretty one, which also adorns nearly all the gardens; it is called in Persian the Goojam or Goojain Arba.

The inhabitants use nothing else for fuel, except the branches and twigs of these trees or the low shrub wood common to the desert, which they, by-the-by, invariably pull out by the roots.

The chase is one of the few amusements the Bokhara people allow themselves. In their steppes they ensnare a great number of foxes and martins, and send the furs to Russia. As they only possess matchlocks, they prefer hawking to shooting. They also use greyhounds, which are black and long-haired, like those in the Crimea.

Nothing could have astonished the natives more than when they saw one of us bring down a bird on the wing, or when we brought down two or three at a time. They ran from all quarters to see us do this, and gave vent to their ecstasy by crying out " Barak Allah, Barak Allah" (Fire God). Their astonishment is very easily understood, as they have never seen shot before; besides this, they have a very roundabout way of firing off one of their pieces. They invariably place their rifles on a tripod or fork, and then have to take some time before their slow matches can ignite the charge.

The fish produce is small; one seldom sees fish of any kind in any of the markets of Bokhara; the few that are caught come mostly from the River Amoo and the Lake of Kara-Kul.

Surrounded by steppes and nomads, Bokhara has plenty of cattle, but the oxen are neither as strong nor as big as those of the Kirghizzees. I cannot tell whether it is an ancient oriental custom, or whether it is done out of economy, but it is nevertheless remarkable, that mutton is the principal kind of meat eaten in this country, and it is the only one to be met with in the market-places. Amongst the Usbeks there exists a tribe called Kukrod, celebrated for bringing up sheep with enormously fat tails, to which the nomads apply the name of " Kindjuk;" sheep are cheaper in the neighbouring districts belonging to Russia: for this reason the Kirghizzees import into Bokhara about 100,000 sheep yearly, which fetch a price of about sixteen rubles; out of this income they buy themselves dresses of silk and cotton, grains, djugera, and peas; the remainder of the produce not used by themselves is sold to great advantage in their native steppes.

The Turcomans import well-shaped horses, full of spirit and of wonderful speed. These stately-looking and well-bred horses, called " Arghamak" by them, vary in price from eight hundred to two thousand five hundred rubles a piece. These same Turcomans, who own large herds of cattle, supply Bokhara with butter, which they bring there in small gourds.

The Bokharians do not work the rich mines that undoubtedly exist in their country, but buy what they require from the Russians. The amount of gold dust found in the bed of the Amoo Daria is not worth mentioning, and I doubt whether gold is to be found in the Zerakhan River, although its name means " Gold Stream."

An important trade is carried on with India and Persia in precious stones. Berdukhan abounds with lapis-lazuli; alum and sulphur are found in quantities round about Samarcand; the best kind of the former comes principally from Mechehed.

The Bokharians are accustomed to little luxury, and have not many requirements; on this account, commerce with the exterior is greater than that of the interior. The coinage of the country consists of gold pieces, silver, and copper; the first are called "tellas," and are larger and heavier than "ducats:" one tella is equivalent to sixteen paper rubles (or 16 francs), or twenty-one tongas; one of the silver pieces is equal to seventy-six copper copeks, or as many centimes. Fifty-five "puhls" of yellow copper, of which each is equal to $1\frac{38}{100}$ copeks or centimes, equal one tonga. All large sums are reckoned in tellas, the smaller ones in tongas and puhls. Seven tellas are equal, in weight, to ten tongas, so that, in Bokhara, the value of silver, compared with that of gold, is as 1 to 14·7 ($14\frac{7}{10}$). Seventy-five tellas weigh the same as one hundred Dutch ducats.

They have several kinds of inscriptions, according to the titles which Mir Hayder has given himself at different times; such as "Padshah Mir Hayder," Amir-ul (Commander of the Faithful), Mir Hyder Sayud, Mir Hyder (Descendant of the Mahomed), "Mir Hyder Amir Damul, Massaine Ghazi" (Prince Daniel, God's Pet, and defender of the faith). "Abul Ghazi Amir Heyder Padshah" (father of the defender of the faith), Emperor Heyder, and lastly, Achmed Caiben Massumi-Ghazi: "on the reverse side of the coin is the inscription Zuriba Bukharai Sharif," i.e., coined in the Holy Bokhara, and the year of the Hejira.

The scientific researches made by M. M. Frahn and Kohler have brought to light a great number of old coins found in Bactriana and the Mavrennahar, and, should the reader be interested in them, I can but refer him to the "Serapis" of the former, and the description in the "Cabinet Asiatique de l'Acadamie des Sciences de St. Petersbourg" of the latter. Most of these coins are found in the ruins on the banks of the Amoo Daria; fortunately the people are beginning to gather them in order to sell them to the Russians, and are gradually refraining from melting them down.

The following Table shows the Bokharian weights and measures as compared with those of France and Russia:—

Bokhara.	Russia.	France.
* Batman = 8 seers ...	8 puds	131,104 kilograms.
One seer = 8 chariks ...	1 pud	16,388 do.
„ charik = 4 nimtshas	5 pounds	2,048 do.
„ nimtshah = 107 mitscals	1 pound 24 soloniksi...	512 grams.
† „ mitscal	112 soloniksi ...	478 do.

* One Batman is about half a camel-load.
† The tella weighs exactly one mitscal, which is the smallest Bokharian weight.

The Bokharian ell, or yard, is called "haze," and is about 107 metres in length. For measuring the coarser cotton stuffs the people use the kar, which equals 321 metres. For measuring land, &c., they possess the tanab, which equals three thousand six hundred (3,600) square feet.

In the whole of Bokhara there does not exist a single large manufactory, and in no one place are more than four or five workmen employed. The preparing of cotton, which is the chief staple of the land, engages a large number of the poor; silk is also spun and prepared here. The fishermen are principally Jews. The Turcomans supply Bokhara with striped shabraques, with pretty good woollen carpets, with camel-hair stuffs, felt, made of goat's hair, which is used for cloaks, and with cherkelle, a kind of stuff of good quality.

The art of tanning is still in its infancy in Bokhara; the leather is far from strong, and this is why so much of that red leather is imported from Russia which is so well known even in Europe. But "Chagrin" (Saomi) is here well made in all colours; it is principally used for overshoes and slippers, which are always either green or black; also for scabbards or sheaths. It is chiefly made out of goat or donkey skin. There are a few celebrated cutlers in Bokhara, who make excellent knives and swords, the best of which are sold sometimes for three tellas; the good Persian blade costs 10 tellas.

Amongst the remaining artizans, the cobblers and shoe-makers are celebrated for the tasteful manner they fix nails into the upper leather of boots and shoes. The saddlers are badly off, as Russia supplies most of their trade.

The Bokharians have the art of dyeing stuffs to perfection, but in other respects their manufactures, &c., are still very inferior. The Bokharian ladies amuse themselves mostly by knitting and sewing; they are fond of hemming their husbands' handkerchiefs and of sending visitors appropriate verses taken from the works of Hafer.

The fine arts are still more behindhand; it is chiefly attributed to the doctrines of Islam, whose dogmas forbid the imitation of any animal or living being. Thus it is easily perceived that the art of painting and sculpture can never attain a high degree of perfection. There are only two or three painters, who do nothing but paint clumsy-looking flowers and other "bizarre" designs on the walls of rooms. In Bokhara I have seen a copy of the celebrated Shahnamah, decorated, and with about fifty illustrations. The colours were hard, the groups or positions were stiff, and the whole of little worth as a work of art, but the details were worked out with the greatest possible care. Several of these illustrations have been copied by Bokharian painters, charging a great price for doing so. Obscene pictures find the greatest sale, and are very much sought after. Sculpturing finds its height in the carving of tombstones, and the present style of architecture is far behind that of three centuries ago, as is witnessed by the splendid domes of the mosques in Samarcand and Bokhara.

The inhabitants of Bokhara give their chief attention to the cultivation of the soil, which they cultivate with the greatest possible care and pains-taking. Moreover, the daily wages for manual labour are very low; carriers would, for instance, move a load of 320 lbs. a distance of a quarter of a mile for the trifling sum of two or three puhls.

During our residence in Bokhara I remarked that the cobblers and shoe-makers complained a great deal about the long spell of fair weather we were enjoying: at this time they did not earn more than 45 (Puhls), 72 centimes, half of which was spent in buying bread, and 10 puhls more for rice, so that these men had to live without meat, and, even then, only had about five sous to pay for their clothing and house rent.

The cheapness of wages would be a great advantage to the starting of large manufactures, but the Bokharians, like the Jews and Tartars, have no idea beyond the occupation of trade.

As regards the trade of Bokhara with other countries, there can be no doubt that circumstances have always been favourable, and that it is daily increasing, thus adding to the wealth of the country.

The power of the Kalifs and the unlimited extension of their dominions could but have a successful influence on the commerce of Central Asia; it was especially during the reign of the Samanides that Bokhara prospered: this is also the epoch from which dates its hitherto unknown and extensive trade, which has even reached as far as China.

This happy result has been mostly attributed to the healthy influence of the Llama religion on the Mongols, the precepts of which recommend mildness, patience, and self-denial, and which have wrought a great change in the character of these people, a change which greatly contributed to the establishment of a peaceable community and the forming of civil laws, especially regarding the rights of property.

Bokhara's flourishing commerce was destroyed by the frequent raids and invasions of Chingis Khan, and did not revive until two centuries later under the fostering care of Timoor, who extended his unlimited protection to the caravans, and sent merchants of influence to all parts of Europe, Arabia, India, and Persia, to collect all sorts of useful information. In those days Bokhara contained, within its walls, merchants of all nationalities; it was acknowledged the chief market town of Central Asia, and the place of meeting for the commerce of the East and of the West. Regardless of the frequent political changes all these countries have undergone, we still find the trade following the same direction.

We read that, already in the days of Alexander the Great, the grand route is mentioned which, up to the present day, is taken by the caravans, and which extends from Bokhara *via* Samarcand to Kashgar, thus passing through the Khanate of Kokan (the Paradise of the Arabs) and over the Takht Suleeman.

The old road joining India and Transoxonia is the same used now-a-days, the chief places of which are Attock, Peshawur, and Cabul. In the same way we find that the roads which in the middle ages served as communications of commerce between the Mavrennahar, Bokhara, and Astrachan, are the very same trodden at this present time by the Bokharian caravans. Thus we find that it is the geographic situation of Bokhara, the nature of its soil, its climate, and the product of neighbouring States, that are the true causes of its commerce, never having been completely extinct, but, on the contrary, always adding to its wealth. To these natural advantages must be added the greed for riches, which is much more marked in the character of the Bokharians than is that of the Tartars generally. The Tajiks have the true merchant spirit, and they show as much sharpness and acuteness in their commercial transactions as frugality, or rather stinginess, in their mode of living. Taking all these circumstances into consideration, it is easily conceived how Bokhara has become exclusively a commercial country.

The thirst after wealth is so intense, that the most respectable State servants follow with hot zeal the occupation of trade, and care nothing for the social opinion that holds the mercantile profession to be less honorable than the one of arms. From the Khan downwards, everybody prefers a money present to any other kind, and this avarice sometimes exceeds all belief. How incredible, for instance, does it seem that at the first audience of M. Negri with the Grand Vizier the sole topic of conversation should have been the value of the presents brought by M. Negri, and that this chief Minister of State should have begged and implored him not to withhold for his own use any of the articles meant as presents for the Khan from the Emperor of Russia. Besides, wealth is here considered to be a virtue; the rich Bokharians receive the title of Beg, which demands respect, or, at least, presumes to do so, and its owner is in the eyes of society an important personage.

The Government has abolished all export duties; the import duties are very light, so that, in this respect, trade may be said to be free. In Bokhara the largest trade has always been carried on more or less with Russia, and even Peter the Great is said to have seen its advantages. It is known that at the time those two expeditions were being formed, one under Prince Bekewitsch Tscherkask, and the other under General Liharer, to take possession of the celebrated gold mines of Vasilkara, that Peter had intended to build a cordon of forts all along the Amoo Daria, thus to open out and strengthen the communications with the East Indies.

General Liharer went up the course of the Totish, as far as three marches beyond North Saysan, but, having lost his way in these boundless steppes, he turned back, and retreated the same way he came, being more fortunate than Prince Bekewitsch, whose tragical end has given rise to the well-known Russian saying, "he is lost like Bekewitsch." Peter had fully determined on establishing a permanent communication with the East Indies and his own possessions, which obliged him first to conquer the Kirghizzees; death prevented the fulfilment of his plans. But, ever since, Russia has always interested herself in the commerce of Central Asia, her chief trade being with Bokhara. In this respect the submission of the lesser Kirghiz hordes in the year 1734 was a great step gained, as also the building of the fort at Orenburg in 1742.

Russian merchants at once accompanied their own caravans as far as Bokhara and Khiva. But the frequent attacks to which they were exposed in the Kirghiz steppes, and especially the destruction of a large Russian caravan in Khiva itself, in the year 1753, frightened them from continuing such a dangerous trade. But the Khivans on their part continued to trade with the Russians, who, in 1762, once more established a commercial association for special trade with Astrachan. In this year also the Khivans sent an Embassy to Russia, followed by a second in 1793. In the following year Katherine II. sent a Doctor Blankenuayel

to the Khan of Khiva, who published a short description of this Khanate.
Since that time our commerce with Khiva has been uninterrupted,
except when, now and then, caravans were attacked. In 1820 General
Zermolow sent Colonel Von Murawief to Khiva, who managed, luckily,
to return quite safe, after having been exposed to a great many personal
dangers.

A Russian caravan was plundered by Puzatshep's band, in 1762,
on the borders of the province of Orenburg, on which account the
Khan of Khiva sent an Embassy to Russia in 1775. Since then, until
1819, eleven ambassadors have made their appearance in Russia, and,
remaining there several years, have managed to secure many advantages
for the commerce of their country from our empire.

The fall of the value of Cashmere shawls, &c., at this time greatly
accelerated this trade. This seems to me to be the right place for making
several remarks and observations on our trade with Central Asia at
the present day. One might have supposed that to have transferred the
Annual Fair of Makaner to Nishni-Novgorod, which was done in 1818,
would also have had some influence in the choice of roads taken by the
numerous Bokharian caravans when coming to Russia, especially as
nine-tenths of their wares were sold at that place, as well as all their pur-
chases were made there. Nevertheless, these caravans, as of old, continue
taking the road of the Russian frontier towns, which lie between the Caspian Sea and Petropolovsk. The shortest road to Nishni-Novgorod would
certainly be *via* Khiva, Saragtechick, Astrachan, and up the Volga, until
they reached the place where the fair is held; but this route is not only
impracticable on account of the scarcity of water, but also because it
necessitates the assumption that the Bokharians and Khivans are on
friendly terms, which is unfortunately not always the case. The longest
way, on the other hand, is *via* Petropolovsk, which is the one usually
chosen by the Bokharians, a choice influenced by the certainty of being
plundered if taking either the road *via* Orenburg, or *via* Troitsk.

Troitsk (in the province of Orenburg) is the frontier town, to which
most of the Bokharian merchants now-a-days wend their way; they find
iron and steel there to be cheaper than in any other of the towns with
which they have come in contact since 1803. The frequency of the
plundering that occurred on the road to Orenburg made them give up
the idea of taking that route, but, after a great deal of trouble, the Military Governor of Orenburg, General Von Essen, succeeded in quieting
and bringing to order the numerous but small hordes who frequented
those parts, so that, after a short time, the merchants once more began
to take the road of Orenburg *via* Astrachan, it being after all the shortest. The time of the arrival and departure of their caravans varies, in a
great measure, with the suitable seasons for passing the large steppes, as
well as with the appointed time of the year for the fair of Nishni-Novgorod, which now generally begins in the middle of July and ends on the
20th August. Generally the caravans leave Bokhara in May, and the
frontiers of Russia in October; sometimes not before November, the
paying of duties, rent, &c., often delaying them. All Bokharian merchants make this journey on horseback, only the servants riding camels,
the latter being so tiring, that even Kirghiz Chieftains always travel,
at least a third of the way, on horseback.

7

The ordinary camel-load is about 16 Puds (262 Kilogrammes); on the average one reckons upon three thousand camels being employed in this trade between Bokhara and Russia* (which by-the-by is much more advantageous to the former than to the latter). The imports from Bokhara are valued yearly at 8 million rubles (in assignments), a very large sum for a population of three and a half millions, thus showing of what importance this trade must be for the country.

Next in importance to that with Russia is the trade with Kashgar; it consists of from seven to eight hundred camel-loads. Besides this, the trade of Bokhara with Cashmere, Cabul, Khokan, with India, Persia, and Afghanistan, is, taking it altogether as regards camel-loads, equal to that with Russia; the total fluctuating commercial capital (chiefly in bank assignments) may be estimated at from 12 to 15 million rubles.

CHAPTER XI.

Interior Economy ; Court ; Clergy ; Administration ; Defences.

The Bokharian Government is a despotic one, but the harshness of its despotism is very much softened down by the influence of religion and by the nomad state of the greater part of the inhabitants of the country.

The Sovereign has the title of Khan, to which he has added the one of "Emir-ulmuminia," or Commander of the Faithful. In his person are combined the heads of all State departments, and he has the power of life and death, and of confiscation of property over all his subjects. Nevertheless, the Mollahs have a great influence on the decisions of the Khan; the greater their piety, the greater their influence. These learned men, who know how to have the "Cherries" and "Kanoons," *i.e.*, the civil religious laws, &c., made for their own advantage, are always called in to the Council by the present Khan whenever there is the least doubt regarding any important matter, and their opinions often decide the doings of this superstitious despot.

The Nomads, who wander about all over the country, could easily leave it altogether, so that their Chiefs are compelled to treat them gently, and have even, sometimes, to flatter them. The present Khan has not had enough regard for this precept, and has therefore lost many Tur-comans, who, having subjected themselves to the Khan of Khiva, show their fidelity by wasting and plundering the countries belonging to their former master. Moreover, the small dimensions of Bokhara prevent the practice of a too rigid despotism. The Hakims or Governors of towns and districts cannot raise themselves to powerful satraps or despots, as was once the case in Persia, neither can they, without the knowledge of the Khan, ill-treat or burden their subjects. The easy access to the capital enables all people of certain standing to lay their private griev-ances before the Khan himself. The present Khan has also introduced

---

* The Bokharian merchants have many privileges; they hardly pay any duties, whilst the Russians have to pay an import duty of 10 per cent. The former estimate their clear profit to be about 30 per cent.

a praiseworthy custom of personally receiving and attending to all complaints made direct to him. Much of the good hereby intended is diminished by the avariciousness of the State officials whom the Khan honors with his confidence; still it prevents the Hakims from carrying on injustice too far.

Notwithstanding this softening down of despotism, which, in practice, is never so hard as it seems in theory, the spirit of the Bokharian Government is of a marked arbitrary character. Indeed, what else can one expect when the mightiest and wealthiest of the land not only call themselves, without any shame, "the slaves of the Khan," but are also proud of bearing this title, and when his real slaves, who have been bought with money, play an important part in possessing his confidence? The slaves of the Koosh-beghi hold important State offices, and it may be said that the whole of the administration is in the hands of the Koosh-beghi family and slaves.

This Minister's father-in-law and one of his nephews are the Governors of Samarcand; one of his brothers is Governor of the fortress Hisagh; another brother holds the title of Inak (Privy Councillor), and has great influence with the Khan. His sons receive pensions without holding any appointment, and one of these, a boy of about fifteen, holds the title of Treasurer to the Khan's private treasury. Thus we find Bokhara presents a repetition of the comedy eventually played by every despotic country, having a Prime Minister possessing unlimited powers, which he either can exercise himself or by his subordinates, who do not possess the noble feeling which we call patriotism.

The mass of Government *employés* in Bokhara must be looked upon as the scum of the population: poverty or ambition are the only true reasons for choosing a calling in which servility on the one hand and favouritism on the other are indispensable conditions for receiving advancement.

A Bokharian who, it can be easily imagined, had never read Montesquieu, said to me one day—"People to whom honor and regard are dear, and also those who have enough to live by, withdraw themselves from Government employment and from the vicinity of the Khan."

The venality of the officials has reached such a point, that both the Khan's favourites, the Koosh-beghi and the Destenvantshi (chamberlain) praise persons who place themselves in such positions that the Khan must perceive them when coming out of the mosque. If such important and wealthy people as these two deign to stoop to such service, then it can be easily understood how it is that, amongst the lower orders, servility should be carried to a marvellous length. The Khan took to himself, during our stay in Bokhara, all the presents brought from the Emperor intended for the chief officers of State.

The story goes that, not long ago, the Khan's eldest son had ordered several rich money changers to be killed in order to have their money vaults ransacked. For this reason the richest and wealthiest unemployed people never make much show; on the contrary, they live as quietly as they can, so as, if possible, to keep the amount of their wealth unknown. This circumstance is the chief reason why luxury is not much indulged in in the capital. The Khan, instead of giving the public Government servants fixed salaries, gives them advantageous commissions; in fact, he gives them permission to squeeze as much out of the people as possible. The whole of this class of vampires aid and abet one another for the sake of their common interest. The senior protects his subordinates, for they facilitate the means of plundering, and all are minor despots, multiplying to a wonderful extent the manifold ways of oppression to which private individuals are exposed.

The Khan, who would outwardly wish to appear as a religious man, gives himself up in private to the most abominable excesses of voluptuousness, and this shameful example is only too often imitated by his courtiers. I shall not here relate the numerous atrocities committed at the time of his ascending the throne; it is apparent that these are too common a part of oriental forms of Government to call for any special notice : moreover, their consequences are everywhere the same.

Suspicion, ever the bugbear of a despot, which allows him no peace, and which never leaves him except when he himself is unconscious, or has utterly forgotten his nature, closely follows the present Khan. He trusts himself to no one except the Koosh-beghi, who has the food destined for the Khan's table cooked and prepared in his own kitchen, and tasted by the cook in his own presence; he tastes it himself, then places it in a vessel, which is sealed up, and afterwards placed before the Khan.

As often as the Khan spends a single night out of Bokhara he obliges his son to accompany him, so great is his mistrust.* We could mention many more traits or peculiarities to complete the description of Bokharian despotism, but we would rather turn away our eyes from such shameful conduct, which can but be lowering to mankind.

It seems that Bokhara has not yet reached such a degree of civilization, that, in it, service with the Khan's person should be looked upon as distinct from that of the State; no Minister has a similar official sphere of activity to that held by the Grand Vizier of Turkey, although the Koosh-beghi may in reality have similar powers.

All business transactions are laid directly before the Khan, an arrangement which is explained by the simplicity of the machinery of administration, as well as by the smallness of the Khanate. The dignity of an Atalik, which the Khan has bestowed upon his father-in-law, the independent Khan of Hissar, can no doubt be compared to that of the Grand Vizier, for its owner is recognized as the first in the land, next to the Khan.

The second place is that of the Commander-in-Chief of the troops, who bears the title of Dadkhwah, or Perwanatshi, and he appears at Court at all large ceremonies.

The third is that of the Sheik-ul-islam, or the head of the clergy; he does not belong to the *personnel* of the Court. An Inak has also an important position, his functions being those of a Privy Councillor or of

---

* The Bokharian law of succession only requires that the successor should belong to the Chinges family: he who can fulfil this condition may ascend the throne.

But it is well known that nothing is more uncertain than an oriental pedigree, and as descent by the female line is valid, there could, of course, be many pretenders who might naturally cause grave disturbances in the country. From this is derived the custom of authorizing every new Khan to put to death or banish all his near relations and their followers.

a Member of the Cabinet.   The Disterhautshi performs the duties of the
Dadkhwah of the master of ceremonies and those of the chamberlain.
Next to these in rank are the Koosh-beghi, who is both Court and State
servant, then the Mir-akhor-bachi, or chief equerry, then Mir-akhor, or
equerry, then the Kari-asker (cari-ordu), or Auditor-General of the
troops, with whom the Khan often has interviews, and who lives in the
palace; then comes the astrologer, the treasurer of the privy purse, then
the Jassul-bachi, with his two hundred Jassools, or policemen, and lastly,
two corps of Guards, of which one has two hundred and twenty men,
who have the rank of officers, called Malram, who may be compared
with our pages at Court; the other contains five hundred men who are
called Cassabardars.

The Khan has in his harem about two hundred women, but they
are not guarded by eunuchs; these last in Bokhara are of no political
importance whatever, and the Khan, either on account of this prosperous
condition, or out of jealousy, has thought it necessary to remove them
from the harem.   As a faithful Mahomedan, he has only four wives, two
of which are his favourites; one of them is the daughter of the Khan of
Hissar, the other a daughter of the Khoja of Samarcand.

The Court of Bokhara does not exhibit much pomp; nevertheless,
the customary ceremonies practised by oriental Princes are punctually
attended to, as was the case at the time of our ceremonial audience.
But in private life the Khan was quite different, and when he met us
in the street he spoke to us, and, on several occasions, conversed in a free
and easy manner with M. deNegri, whilst holding a private audience.
Once a week he rides on horseback to the convent of Bogowodin to say
his prayers, accompanied by a small detachment of his guards; the way
being led by Jassools, who make room for him with their white sticks.
All who meet him stand still, bow, and cry out salaam-alaikum, which
greeting is responded to by an officer who rides in front.

On Fridays he also rides on horseback to a mosque, distant about
fifty paces from his seraglio, when he is followed by his State officers on
foot.   On his passing through his palace gate the guard drawn up in
line throw themselves on the ground, offering a salute, which is also
acknowledged by an officer in his retinue.   This ceremony in itself is
imposing.

In Bokhara it is a source of great astonishment that a Tajik should
play an important role at Court.   He is the Disterhautshi, who from his
early youth has known how to win the Khan's favour by his devoted
attachment, and who now has as great an influence with the Khan as has
the Koosh-beghi.   These two rivals " manage " one another with an
" address " which would bring credit on the most civilized courtiers of an
ancient *régime*.   Moreover, the Court of Bokhara, as well as that of
many others, is never in want of intrigues and cabals.

There further exists in Bokhara, under the name of a Divan, a
kind of Council, which only assembles after special notice, and of which
the Khan is invariably the President; its members are chosen quite
optionally by the Khan, and no office of State in itself entitles the
holder of it to be a member of this Council.   It consists of from five to
twenty members, and it directs the most important business and affairs

of the State. The dignitaries generally form its members, and the opinions of the clergy are of great weight at its sittings, as it generally manages to back its opinion by some religious precept.

The Bokharian clergy form a hierarchy with the Sheik-ul-islam for its head. He has the giving of all preferments, and is often appealed to in very important cases, so that the judicial verdicts may be in keeping with the laws of religion. Next to him in rank is the Alam, next to him are the Muftis, then the Dana-Mollahs, or learned priests, and lastly, the Akhoons, or common priests. The title of Mollah, or member of clergy, is also given to a Jew who can read. In former days the clergy were of no important political influence, and it is hardly a quarter of a century since that the then reigning Khan, who particularly favoured the army, had the clergy as it were proscribed. The present Khan though, who is very pious, follows a different system altogether; he has largely increased their number, and has endowed them munificently, so that now, in Bokhara alone, their number exceeds two thousand.

He further favours and protects them at every opportunity, so that, should several of his successors imitate his example, the priesthood would in course of time gain a great influence in the affairs of the State, especially as the people are excessively ignorant and fanatical. At present the reigning caste of Uzbeks, who are more warlike than pious, are, however, held in greater respect than the priesthood. Moreover, we must further remark that, in Bokhara, those who are learned in divinity and in law form a corporation of their own, which is perfectly independent of any other authority.

All towns of any importance have a Cazi, or Judge; the smaller ones only a Rais, or Police Commissioner. Judicial proceedings are carried on very rapidly. The parties appear in person, and two witnesses suffice to prove a case, and are considered enough to direct the Cazi or Rais in his judgment.

The Judge of Bokhara bears the title of Cazi Kalan (Chief Justice), but it does not necessitate his having any command over the other Judges; still he is considered more important, as, being near the Khan, he has often to decide cases of importance. He has in his Office two Muftis, who receive money compensation for the time occupied in affixing their seals, which act renders a decree valid.

The Cazis of other towns have only one Mufti, who is subordinate to them, and is of nearly no consequence at all. It is allowable to appeal to the Khan from the decree of a Cazi, but here, as elsewhere, the art of justifying the Cazi's verdict is well known, for the official constantly declares the seal of his Mufti to have been forged, and frequently brings the case once more before his bench, thereby increasing the amount of his income.

The custom of removing the Cazis after holding office for eighteen months, as is the case in other Mahomedan countries where fear is entertained of their exerting an influence dangerous to their Government, does not exist in Bokhara.

It is easily conceived that in a land where bribery is so common that the Rais, who has the power of fining, should do so arbitrarily, thus adding a good deal to his income. A Jew who, during our stay in Bokhara, had sold some brandy to one of our Cossacks, had been thrown into prison by order of one of the Raises, and although the Jew had already received sixty lashes, the Rais still had himself paid a hundred and fifty Tellas by the Israelite's family. The corporal punishment administered was exceedingly severe, the sticks used being very thick, and being laid on unmercifully on the stomach as well as on the back : seventy-five cuts with these are considered equal to capital punishment. A still more cruel punishment consists in placing the culprit bound hand and foot in a room filled with a kind of flying insect, whose sting is excessively painful. This punishment takes the place of torture : a person on whom it is inflicted does not survive the third day.

The organization of the army, the administration of finance, and the sources of the Khan's income, are, in Bokhara, closely connected. The land is looked upon as the conqueror's own, who tries to make the most out of it he can, while, in order to possess an army, he has only to subject himself to religious rites and to make the proper quantity of sacrifices. The feudal system can be said to exist to a certain extent, as lands are mostly lent as rewards for military services.

The greater part of the Khan's income is derived from his own estates. The keeping up of his troops is the greatest item in his expenditure, for, as in Turkey, his own troops are mercenaries, and those who have received grants of land, and who thus form the militia, or landwehr, take active service only when there is a general summons.

The necessity for properly dividing the estates and grants of land and for securing order and a good administration has caused Bokhara to be divided into forts or districts, of which Bokhara, Samarcand, Siawudin, and Kara-Kul are the largest, and Tshalak and Nuratagh the smallest. At the head of each Tumen or district is placed a Hakim; his pay consists of what he clears by his tenancy. The Tumen of Samarcand is rented for 300,000 Batmans (about 39,300,000 Kilogrammes) of wheat and 500,000 Tongas (380,000 francs) in cash; that of Siawudin for 1,000,000 Batmans wheat and 100,000 Tongas; that of Kara-Kul for 25,000 Tellas; the two small ones of Tshalak and Nuratagh each for 4,000 Batmans of wheat and 20,000 Tongas. The total income of these domains may be estimated at about 10 million francs, of which only half go to the treasury, the Hakim having to pay with the other half for his own district officials and for the maintenance of the troops quartered on his estate. There are even a few districts in which the Hakim has to spend more than the income derived therefrom; this is the case, for instance, in Uratepah and in other frontier towns, which contain necessarily a very large garrison.

The taxes and income of the domains are collected by the Hakims; they either rent the farms to the highest bidder, or else take two-fifths of the produce to themselves : this system naturally calls for very strict supervision.

It is therefore customary to send some Jassools or Diwan-beghis, or Murzas to the farms, to estimate the produce of the land and to collect their share. The Jassools and the Diwan-begis are police officers; the Murzas are writers or clerks; and the real tax-gatherers are called Mighter.

The office of Hakim brings with it very high rank, because the Hakims are in direct communication with the Khan, whose favour they endeavour to gain by numerous presents, principally of rice, horses, and sometimes even money.

The import duties have already been mentioned : if the value of the imports is estimated at fifteen million francs, then the income derived must be about 400,000 francs, which is expended in the keeping up of the schools and clergy.

Besides this, there is another tax of two and a half per cent. on the merchandize which is exempt from import duty, and, further, those taxes levied on the natural productions, as, for instance, on dried manna, used for preserving fruits, shaffelles, &c., which bring in an income of about 15,000 francs. The Koosh-beghi is Director-General of all import duties and taxes, and in this has as many opportunities of enriching himself as well as influence on commerce in general and on the foreign affairs of Bokhara. The Bokharians have also to pay a tenth, called Tikat or Uchr, which the Koran requires to be spent in alms. Every Bokharian whose income is more than three hundred tongas has to give up the tenth of it either in money or grain; also, out of forty sheep, he has to give up one, out of an hundred, two, out of three hundred, four, out of four hundred, six, and so on. To this are also subject all the nomad Turcomans, who recognize the Khan as their Sovereign.

Four wood lands near Joitshi, five near Charjooi, as many near Hiski, and four near Ukarzoom on the Amoo, are let by Government, and bring in an income of a couple of thousand rubles.

On comparing the total income with the Khan's expenditure for keeping up his Government and troops, there remains for his private use about one million rubles, which, judging by the want of comfort and the absence of luxury in his surroundings, is far beyond his requirements.

The finance administration is entirely in the hands of the Koosh-beghi and of the Khan, and is in itself as simple as the other administration.

The armed force consists only of cavalry, and is composed either of liege vassals or of mercenary troops. The latter form the standing army, and are about 25,000 strong; the number of those vassals who only join on special occasions is more than 60,000. The Khan could send from 12 to 13,000 troops on an expedition at a time, the remainder being required to man the fortresses on the frontier; the most important of these are Uratepah, Jisagh, Samarcand, Kara-Kul, and Karchi, all of which demand strong garrisons.

During our stay in Bokhara the Khan sent an expedition of twelve thousand men to punish an Uzbek Chief, who had taken possession of the town of Balkh, which was subject to the Khan. Soon after our departure the Khivans made a raid into Bokhara and sacked Jarjoo. Although Bokhara is more powerful than the neighbouring States, it is not able to enforce respect amongst them, the reason of which lies either in the Khan's pusillanimity or in the warlike spirit of his neighbours.

The Bokharian soldiers are called Sipahis or Caraalamans; their pay is about six Tellas, one Tella for hay, five Batmans Jugera, and as much wheat. The Casserbardars (Khassbardars), or guardsmen, receive double pay. Their officers are the Dah-bashi, or Commander of ten men, the Tshur-agasi, or non-commissioned officer, the Jooz-bashi, or leader of one hundred men, the Terash-bashi, or Lieutenant, the Pasand-bashi, or

Commander of 500 men, the Tuksabai or Regimental Chief, the Kur-
ghanbeghi or Brigadier-General, the Dadkhwah or Divisional General,
and the Perwanatshi, the Commander of the Army or Field Marshal.

All officers or leaders have the title of Sarkardeh, and receive pay
either in money or in grain. The troops of five hundred men belonging
to the Pasand-bashi have for a distinction a small flag called Bayrak.
Each Regiment of 1,000 men has a large colour called Tugh, which is
carried by the Mir-bashi, who holds a very exalted rank.

The Sipahis' weapons consist of a matchlock, a very long lance,
and a crooked sword, like those of the Persians. A few wear a shirt
of mail, a steel helmet, and carry a round shield of buffalo hide. The
artillery consists of about ten Persian Guns, only three or four of which
have carriages; although they have only three wheels, still they are very
difficult to move and to use, and are by no means creditable to the
Topchi-bashi, or Artillery Chief, who, by-the-by, is an old Russian
soldier.

Once a year the Khan reviews his troops, generally in the neighbourhood of Bogowodin, which review usually lasts about a fortnight.
The *élite* of the army is formed by the Uzbeks, a warlike people. They
fight without any discipline, and always for themselves, or as allies; they
possess handsome horses. The most daring horsemen ride out as
skirmishers, often engaging in single combat; this is followed by a general
attack and *mêlée*. These engagements are very short, for the horses are
so fleet, that they are of immense advantage to the worsted party. As
these expeditions are carried into barren countries without stores, &c.,
the hordes look upon a three weeks' campaign as something unusual, so
that they are after all nothing but raids.

As regards foreign affairs, Bokhara does not in the least trouble
itself to have the neighbouring Khanates as allies, for it neither fears
them nor requires their aid. The present political state of Central Asia
can be well compared to that of Europe before the sixteenth century,
when the custom of having Ambassadors at Foreign Courts was still
unknown.

Amongst the neighbouring States of Bokhara, the Khanate of Khiva
is the most troublesome, as its nomad hordes often make raids into
and plunder the country round about: its Chief is an avaricious and
warlike man. For centuries the two countries have been at enmity with
one another. Khiva has on several occasions been conquered by the
Bokharians, but has each time succeeded in regaining its freedom. Ten
years ago it was taken possession of by Emir Hayder, but from religious
scruples he gave it back its independence, as the Koran forbids true
believers from taking or conquering one another's possessions without
good cause. Lately, a more marked hatred has sprung up between
them on account of some Khivans having plundered a caravan.

The Uzbeks are burning to revenge this insult with the blood of
their enemies, but the Emir-ul-muminia believes that to destroy Khiva
would be to destroy a member of the whole family to which he belongs;
he thus, through indulgence and superstition, remains equally negligent
of acquiring a warlike renown as he is about the welfare of his subjects.

The Khan of Khokan, who is connected with him by ties of relation-
ship, is partly guided by his political views. There seems to be a good

understanding between him and the Khan of Bokhara. On account of the latter's power, and also for the sake of commercial interest, he is far from wishing to break it.

The Khan of Hissar is his son-in-law's (Emir Hayder's) staunchest ally. This Khanate is completely surrounded by Bokharian territory, but it is also so situated, that it can be easily inundated, thus affording a good protection against attacks from the Uzbeks. Besides, all these small Khanates manage to retain their independence.

Although Bokhara has commercial communications with Persia, Afghanistan, India, Cashmere, and Kashgar and Little Thibet, still the political relations with these countries, under the present Khan, are of no moment whatever.

Since his ascending the throne, twenty years ago, his relations with Kashgar have been restricted to having once sent the Commander of the town a letter with several presents. He has never had any friendly negotiation with the Shah of Persia; on the contrary, his hatred towards him is most bitter, partly because he belongs to a different religious sect, partly because his dissatisfied subjects find an asylum in Persia, and, lastly, also because the Persians execrate the Bokharians for their keeping, as before mentioned, more than thirty thousand of their compatriots in the severest bonds of slavery.

Every year the Khan of Bokhara sends a pious Mahomedan of the Sunite sect to the Padshah at Constantinople, the representative and successor of the Khalif, with a large sum of money, besides assurances of respect, friendship, and attachment. In 1818 the Grand Sultan sent him in return an Ambassador and a few scientific books as presents, with which the Khan was very much pleased.

For the last fifty years hardly one year passed without the Russian Government having had occasion to send an answer or intimation to the Bokharian diplomatists. These latter are generally merchants; their own interest as well as that of the Prime Minister induces them to ask for credentials and the title of an Ambassador, as they are thus enabled to pass all their merchandize into Russia without duty. Moreover, when the Khan has any business to transact with a neighbouring State, he always makes use of merchants to carry his despatches.

Altogether, on account of the Khan's indifference, the foreign political relations of Bokhara are unimportant. As long as his own income is not interfered with, he is perfectly satisfied: never troubling himself about the affairs of the country—he allows them to take their own course.

CHAPTER XIV.

Customs and manners. Civilization.

The population of Bókhara is composed partly of nomads and partly of permanent residents, some of the latter being citizens, others country people: on this account it is but natural that their customs and manners should differ in some respects. I have only been thrown in contact with the resident population, and must confine my remarks to them; besides, nomad life is the same in all Mahomedan countries, and hardly requires to be especially noticed. But I must to a certain extent contradict the report, which has been received all over Europe, that the nomads are stealers of men. The protection given by Government to commerce, a certain regular administration, lastly, the prescribed laws of the Koran, which forbids any true believer to have a faithful as a slave, have to a great extent stopped the custom of man-stealing in Bokhara.

Hindoos, Persians, Russians, and Armenians can all travel in Bokhara with safety as soon as the Government is satisfied as to their being *bond fide* merchants. Prisoners are only made in time of war, and is principally by the Uzbeks and Turcomans from the District of Mawri, who make inroads into Khorassan.

On account of their religion having such a great influence over the domestic life of the people, we find that all Mahomedan nations have very much the same social customs and manners. The Uzbeks especially are true Turks, and their mode of living is very similar to that of the Osmanlis in Constantinople, for everything that is done by the Khalif and everything that takes place in Stamboul is much admired by them.

A Mussulman believes himself to be pure and free from blame as soon as he has submitted to the precepts contained in the Koran and to its commentaries; besides, he knows nothing of those holiest of laws which are dictated by honor and conscience. The Bokharians are very superstitious, and the Government does not fail to strengthen them in their ways of thinking. The law which prohibits Kaffirs from wearing clothes similar to those worn by the faithful exists in Bokhara. The Government encourages the proselytes and regenerators very much. Nearly all slaves are forced to give themselves out to be Mahomedans; they are obliged to wear a turban, and are circumcised, whether they like it or not, so that they at least may have the outward distinction of the professors of the Islam religion. The pious Bokharian believes himself sullied should he touch anything presented to him by a Kaffir. During our stay in Bokhara the children used sometimes to greet us with the usual Salaam-alaikum, for which I have often heard their elders curse them, admonishing them severely for welcoming unbelievers with a salaam.

Intolerance and superstition are so great in Bokhara, that it is not to be wondered at that the unbelievers living there have to pay extra taxes, and that they are exposed to an excess of oppression and injustice.

Besides, the spirit of the Government is such, that no other religion than the Mahomedan could ever exist in this country; for this reason we find there no Gebers or historians: only the Jews through excessive submissiveness and craftiness have been able to keep their own written history.

This Government does not look upon prayer as a mere private obligation, but also as a public duty, and is not merely satisfied with distributing justice, but insists upon having, although contrary to the true Mahomedan religion, the guidance of the religious behaviour of private individuals. Every house-owner is obliged to attend prayers in the mosque every morning, the Police officers taking the names from the door-keepers of each mosque of all who are absent, and then calling on them in their own houses and belabouring them with sticks.

According to a standing order, as may be seen any day at four in the afternoon in the Redjistan, or large market-place, two policemen are told off to drive all the merchants and vendors into the nearest mosque, this being the holy hour; accordingly, they charge into the crowd, which at this time is at its height, with whips three fingers thick, and deal out blows right and left quite indiscriminately: this of course always causes a great uproar; some cry out, others shriek with laughter, all take to their heels, and in one moment the booths, tables, and tents disappear, and the mosques are crowded with pious Mussulmen who have been driven in with blows to say their prayers.

All the superstitions common to Mahomedans are to be met with in Bokhara, hence astrology is held in honor. The Khan has a Court Astrologer, who has studied his art in Ispahan. The custom of killing a goat in memory of a friend, an honored person, or a saint, exists here as well as amongst the Kirghizzees. The props and supports of the roof in one of the colonnades in the mosque of Bogowodin are decorated with the skins of innumerable goats, horses, &c., which have been sacrificed in honor of some saint or other.

If superstitious customs are still to be met with amongst Europeans, it is not astonishing to find them amongst such people as the Bokharians. Not knowing the use of cards, although they must have seen them amongst Persians and Hindoos, they use dice in foretelling events. Four being placed upon an iron rod are spun round: the numbers displayed are rapidly interpreted by the Bokharians, who are adepts in the law of chances and probability. Few Bokharians smoke, for it is written in the Koran that it is unlawful to take anything inebriating in one's mouth. This religious scruple greatly irritated a certain Turkish messenger, who, on entering the town, demanded his pipe to show his contempt for it. The Persian slaves smoke a great deal, and always use the kalian, a kind of pipe in which the smoke is led by a tube through water. I have also often seen them dig two conveying holes in the ground, into one of which they placed tobacco, the other being used for inhaling the fumes: this ingenious plan serves them well when in want of a pipe.

As is well known, the drinking of strong drinks is strictly forbidden in all Mahomedan countries; for this very reason they have the greater charm for the young and rich. There are a great number of Bokharians who indulge to excess in private, but one never sees a drunken man in the streets, for he would be in danger of his life. The Koosh-beghi himself has frankly owned to us that, in former years, he and the Khan had often got inebriated together. Towra Khan, the heir apparent to the throne, finding the wine of Bokhara not good enough, gets intoxicated every evening with opium. This Prince, who, it is said, had formerly been rather clever and accomplished, has, since he has taken to this pernicious habit, lost all energy and vital power.

One of the Khan's sons, hearing that M. de Negri was to have an audience with his father on a certain occasion, and knowing that we always drink wine, begged and entreated him to get drunk before appearing in the Khan's presence.

The presence of courtezans and paramours is prohibited in Bokhara. They were expelled about thirty years ago by the present Khan's father: they were chiefly gipsy girls (Tschinghaneh). Adultery is here punishable with death.

I once asked a young Bokharian of good family of what his amusements consisted; he said that he gave midday dinner parties accompanied by the music of his slaves; further, that he sometimes attended the chase; and, lastly, that he kept Jawanis or boy favourites. The calm and unhesitating way he told me this astonished me, and proved to me how well acquainted they are here with the most horrible of all vices.

The Khanates of Asia entertain a slave trade with the Kirghizzees and Turcomans, which is mostly kept up by the raids of both of these nomad hordes, and by war with the Persians. It has already been mentioned that the occupation of Malwa has increased the number of Persian slaves in Bokhara by twenty-five thousand, thus making all in all about forty thousand. From five to six hundred Russians are kept in miserable slavery, sold originally by the Khivans, Kirghizzees, or Turcomans, who make use of all fishermen stranded on the eastern coast of the Caspian Sea as slaves.

Besides, we find among the slaves in Bokhara Hezurehs, Chitrars, Siapuchs, and even Georgians; their number never diminishes, for they are given Persian women in marriage, it being the interest of their masters to keep them up. The price of a well-built man is about 40 or 50 Tellas (640 to 800 Francs). Should he be acquainted with any profession, such as turning, making shoes, or the work of a blacksmith, then his value increases to about 100 Tellas (16,000 Francs). The women, as a rule, are cheaper than the men, except those still young and handsome; they are sometimes sold for 100 to 150 Tellas (2,400 Francs). The lot of a slave in Bokhara is terrible to think of; the Russians unanimously complained of being stinted in food, and of being beaten most unmercifully.

I remember seeing one whose master had cut off his ears, pierced his hands with nails, and, taking the skin off his back, had poured boiling oil on his arms, so as to force him to tell by what means a comrade of his had escaped.

One day the Koosh-beghi found one of his Russian slaves intoxicated; the next day he had him brought on to the Redjistan to have him hung. On reaching the gallows this unfortunate was offered forgiveness if he would disown his Christian religion, but he preferred dying a martyr for his faith.

Most of the Russian slaves in Bokhara were kept in confinement during a whole week before our departure with chains bound to their ancles; and only one managed to escape to us, and he, after runing about for a week in the wilderness, joined us about a hundred versts distant from Bokhara. It would be quite impossible for me to describe the joy of those Russian slaves whose freedom we bought, now and then, on our way. Is it possible to believe that the Bokharian Government wanted to prevent these released slaves from returning to their homes in Russia? This fanatic Government even forbade its subjects to sell us any Russian slaves, giving, as a pretext, that the number of possible proselytes would be greatly reduced. I cannot let this opportunity pass without expressing a hope that Russia will retaliate on the Bokharians and Khivans by seizing their property, and not desist until every one of her subjects has been released from slavery: this measure, though severe, would be far from being unjust, and thousands of Russians, who have been robbed of their country, their families, and their religion, would have these restored to them.

The wealthy Bokharians possess generally about 40 slaves, but some of the most distinguished, as, for instance, the Koosh-beghi, have about a hundred, for they require a large retinue, and have, besides, many gardens and much land, demanding a greater number of hands to labour.

There is not, I think, a single Bokharian citizen who is in easy circumstances that does not possess a garden and a villa outside the town, in which he spends the hot days of the summer.

Owners of land let their property, or else have it worked by slaves. The more refined enjoyments of life, homely comfort, and the pleasures of society are perfectly unknown in Bokhara. During the winter time the houses are cold and damp, and contain no other furniture than carpets, blankets, &c. The only enjoyment indulged in is that of the harem. No large meetings of society, no feast of any kind, ever interrupts the quiet monotony of a Bokharian existence.

I have never seen dancing, except once round a sick man, the time being marked by beating the hands together and singing " bala kibla," just like the Circassians; but these last use the sylables " a-pu-pa-pu-pa."

The Persian civilization, introduced into Bokhara by Timoor, is still to be traced in a few of the ceremonies now in existence. After the death of the Koosh-beghi's first wife, who was very much respected by all Mahomedans, the principal inhabitants of Bokhara paid him visits of condolence; at the same time the Koosh-beghi distributed presents to his late wife's surviving relations, whom he also fed for several days after. A Bokharian when paying another a visit never departs without asking his host's permission to do so, who invariably offers him tea, fruit, and comfits. It is considered a still greater politeness if he is given some of these to take home with him. As often as we paid the Koosh-beghi a visit, he each time offered us sweetmeats and cakes, which he always had sent after us to our houses. The Khan himself also makes presents of sweets, sometimes accompanied by a whole suit of clothes, which in Bokhara is called a " Sarpay." Before entering the apartments of a married man, it is customary to wait outside the door for a few minutes, so as to give the women time to withdraw. The most respectful way of sitting is by squatting on one's heels, and if one wishes to be more comfortable, one may cross one's legs.

When greeting one another, the Bokharians place the right hand on their chest and say " Khosh." These civilities are often exaggerated in the most ludicrous manner by the Persian slaves, who, by-the-by, are wonderful mimics.

On the whole, the Bokharians, especially the Tajiks, are polite, complaisant, and sometimes even cringing: this politeness was the more striking to us, as we had, only three weeks before, been with the Kirghizzees, who are invariably rude and abrupt.

Bokharian diet is very simple; after morning prayers they drink tea prepared with milk and salt, making a kind of soup; they generally dine at four or five, and they seldom have anything beyond a pilao, which consists of rice, beet-root, and mutton.

Immediately after dinner they drink tea, prepared as in Europe. Coffee is not much used in Bokhara. They eat with their fingers, and spoons and forks are unknown to them.

Their apparel usually consists of two long blue-striped cotton garments, one of which being shorter and lighter than the other forms a shirt. They all wear a turban of calico from fifteen to twenty feet in length. Many Uzbeks only wear a red cloth cap, which runs up into a point, and is bound with martin skin. In Bokhara, as in Constantinople, the rank and position of the wearer is distinguished by the colour of the turban. All inhabitants wear short light drawers beneath their loose white trowsers, which either through laziness or bashfulness they never change. Wealthy people wear khilats of half silk and half cloth; the rich government officials bedeck themselves with Cashmere shawls and gold embroidery, also according to their rank. These glittering garments, the spotless white turban, and the thick bushy beards of the courtiers, made a remarkable impression on us at our first audience.

In the streets the women wear a long cloak, the sleeves being tied behind their backs and a black veil, which completely hides their faces. They cannot well see through them, and whenever we passed them, they slily lifted up a corner. The wives of the Tajiks also found a great delight in showing us their beautiful black eyes. Altogether the ladies of Bokhara seem to have started the fashion of taking a good view of the Franks; the remotest part of our flat roof was their chief place of congregation, as well as the boundary of their curiosity prescribed by their sense of decorum. Here, less perceived by the Bokharians, we had opportunities of admiring handsome women, with black eyes full of fire, and splendid teeth, and a very pretty complexion. Bokharian surveillance soon put a stop to this worldliness; the women were prevented from ascending the roofs, and we were thus deprived of the pleasure of witnessing a scene which had often given a great relish to our appetites. How is it possible that such handsome women should disfigure themselves by wearing rings through their noses, and by painting their cheeks, when nature has blessed them with so many charms? The women and some of the men colour their finger nails with the red juice of henna, a plant which for this purpose is pressed.

The Persians use this stuff, too, for colouring their beards first red, so as better to take the black colour, which they apply a little later. I have seen white hair the tips of which were dyed with this dye. The women paint their eyebrows black and join them with similar colour; they also paint their eyelashes and the edge of the eyelid black with surmah or galena brought from Cabul.

This is also done by a few Bokharians and Hindoos. Elegant Bokharians (dandies) cause all hair, excepting that of the beard, to be plucked out from their cheeks, and one can often see barbers thus occupied from the street.

The influence of nomad life is observable in the want of vehicles in Bokhara. There is no other kind of equipage than the common cart before mentioned, which can never be used for driving or travelling: for this only camels, horses, mules, and donkeys are employed. Horses sometimes carry a whole family, and children are taught to ride from their infancy, thus laying the foundation for their becoming good riders. The Khan's wives were the only ones I saw make use of mules; they sat two and two on each beast.

They have the privilege, as well as all other married women, of making calls in the city. When a man of easy circumstances rides on horseback, he is always followed by a man on foot; the rich man uses for this purpose his slaves, and it is saddening to see the slaves gasping and breathlessly following their master, who generally rides very fast; the poorer man makes his son ride behind him, and usually rides at a slow pace.

From this short sketch of the customs and manners of the Bokharians, we see that luxury is limited within very narrow bounds; clothes and horses are the only articles with which they try to make a show. Their Persian carpets are of inferior quality; they hardly have any furniture: one never sees them keeping a clock, and only very seldom a watch: they have no silver articles, no glass panes in the windows of their badly-built houses, and they are perfectly unacquainted with comforts and enjoyments which are by us regarded as of great importance. The reasons for this are partly a want of civilization, partly fear of displaying their riches in such a despotic country, and partly the avarice, which is considered the Bokharian's besetting sin: still it may be expected that an intercourse with Russia and India will give rise to the desire for more comfort and luxury.

Bokhara's ancient renown as a learned city proves that it must have been the centre of enlightenment in former times. This was, no doubt, due to her commerce and wealth, invariably the pioneers of civilization. Europe owes her progress principally to the favourable configuration of her sea-board. With respect to trading at sea, we find something analogous in Bokhara, in so far as caravans can be compared with fleets at sea, and that for centuries they have always taken the same course across the deserts. Bokhara's splendour under the dynasty of the Samanides is well known (896 to 998 A.D.), as well as her progress in sciences during the twelfth century.

In this respect Samarcand was still better known, and only expired with the downfall of the Ghazee (1184). Timoor, who is said to have had a taste for science and art, had called together in Mavrennahar all the savants of his immense empire, and an entirely new civilization sprung up in this conqueror's native land. At the present time scholastic knowledge of theology holds the first rank in the sciences taught in Bokhara, or rather it is the only one to which attention is at all bestowed. The colleges are filled with students and scholars, who spend ten, twenty, yea, even thirty years, in studying the commentaries on the Koran, thus wasting the best years of their lives without improving themselves. When their memory is crowded with small things of no consequence they are called Mudiris or Mollahs, and, proud of their fruitless knowledge, they look down with pity on those who are ignorant of them.

Idle discussions regarding the meaning of the texts in the Koran, the enunciation of thesis which no one dares to question, and the pondering over more or less true copies of Aristotle, constitute the occupations of a Bokharian philosopher.

The Khan often starts a question in theology which Mudians assemble to discuss. A sharp and clever Mudiri one day ventured to contradict the accepted opinions, and began to prove his own views with wonderful precision. Instead of answering him, the ulemas ordered him to be silent, unless he wished to be precipitated from the top of the highest minaret: of course such a threat put an end to all discussions.

Like all Mahomedan people, they attach great importance to medicine, which, with them, is mixed up a great deal with chemistry and all sorts of superstitious quackeries. The practice of medicine can, however, never improve among them, for they blindly hold up the oldest books on the subject as their authorities. A good Bokharian physician is expected to be able to guess a patient's malady on merely touching his pulse.

The doctors here look upon physical constitutions to be of four kinds—cold and warm, dry and moist, and accordingly their medicines are heating, freshening, weakening, and strengthening. Moreover, the doctors know nothing of anatomy or physiology beyond the knowledge of arteries, which they divide into those of the head, the chest, and the abdomen. To the best of my belief these same ideas existed in Europe only a few centuries ago.

Astronomy, as already mentioned, is in Bokhara closely connected with astrology. The Khan's astrologer, for instance, has to give him notice at least two days before any eclipse, &c., so as to enable people to prepare for these fear-awakening phenomena in proper time.

The present astrologer in Bokhara (there is only one) is able to reckon the moon's orbit; on the other hand, he believes the sun to be moving round the world, considers that the tail of a comet is formed by the concussion of two planets, and that there exist only five planets. Moreover, he is a great admirer of the Ptolemaic system, and looks upon the ancient Bokharian Astronomer Oluj-bej as infallible.

The most educated Bokharians have but a limited knowledge of geography, and geographic charts would have been perfectly unknown to them, had not a merchant brought over a few from Russia, for which they do not seem to care much. Even the Prime Minister has not the slightest idea regarding them.

It is the same with the knowledge of history. The bigoted Mollahs look upon it as a profane and useless study, and the laity study it merely as an amusement. Exception must be made of certain books, such as the history of Alexander the Great, which is generally liked. A Mollah, told off by the Khan, has to read this book out loud in the public market-place; he is often listened to by a large crowd, who, at the end of his reading, collect some small sum for him as a reward.

In spite of the large number of schools and colleges that exist in Bokhara, the greater part of the people can neither read nor write. But most of the Todjik merchants, seeing that so much is essential for the successful issue of commerce, are beginning to make their children attend school regularly. A few of these attend the colleges, but as Tadjiks are universally despised, it is seldom that one of them ever attains a distinguished post among the clergy.

The children of the most respectable people never learn anything more than how to read and write, and to learn by heart a few passages in the Koran. The Khan's children have private tutors; he himself teaches them the Koran, in assemblies of sometimes three hundred spectators.

The languages mostly spoken in Bokhara are Arabic and Persian; the latter being the language of the Tadjiks and all civilized Bokharians: it is also the one used in correspondence and business. The idiom generally used in Bokhara differs but slightly from the pure Persian. The Turkish language is remarkable for its harshness, and is only spoken by the Nomad Uzbeks and Turcomans; it sounds very much like the language spoken by Kirghizzees and Russian Tartars.

The endowment of schools is here looked upon as a virtue, the maintenance of scholars a duty, and all the income derived from taxation has to be distributed amongst the Mollahs, Mudiris, scholars, and the poor. This established law is strictly kept by the present Khan, who pays the Mudiris from a hundred to two hundred tellas, and the students three hundred tongas each. He also often distributes prizes amongst the boys, which are in value proportional to the position of the scholar in his class or school.

It is even customary that the rich and wealthy present the tabibs, or students, who often make their appearance unasked, with a dinner and a small present, which is here called a Sadakat or Khayrat. Timoor endowed several colleges with land property, the tenth part of the produce of which he divided amongst the pupils.

From the above it is easy to understand how there can be ten thousand students in Bokhara, who partly live in the mosques and colleges, and partly with private tutors; but if amongst such a number of individuals, who devote themselves solely to the acquirement of knowledge, there is not one who takes the right road to do so, the reason of such folly can but be discovered in the prejudice and fanaticism fostered by the Mahomedan religion. It is hard to believe that, in the whole of Bokhara, there does not exist one library containing more than three hundred volumes; the one belonging to the Khan contains only two hundred, and in many colleges there are none at all. Moreover, it is remarkable that Shah Mira-beg, who favoured the Military, appropriated to himself the income of four hundred Mudiris, and greatly diminished the number of Mollahs. This circumstance proves that the influence of the ulemas is not paramount, and that great reforms could be achieved. A Bokharian Prince, sufficiently enlightened, therefore, could have a beneficent influence on Central Asia, and could once more return to it that civilisation, improved by the advancement of centuries, which originally came from Europe. The progress of culture in Russia demands that such an idea should be carried out in this vast empire. Russia is the country whose duty it is to impart to the Khanates of Central Asia a healthy moral impulse and to spread in these countries the benefits of European civilization.

APPENDIX I.

Regarding the trading route from Semipalatinsk to Cashmere viâ the towns of Ileh, Aksoo, Yarkand, and Thibet. Translated from Persian manuscript by Professor J. Seukowski of St. Petersburg.

Our learned oriental linguist, M. Councillor C. Frahn, has had the kindness to send me the original of the following treatise written in the Persian language, which he managed to procure during his stay in Kasan, and I believe this to be the most favourable opportunity of giving publicity to it, adding it to the foregoing work of the Baron bon Meyendorff with his kind permission. The description of this trading route may have been given by a Bokharian merchant, as can be easily traced in the curious idiomatic expressions as well as in the orthography used. Moreover, it can be seen that the author was a man who could not write, as is generally the case with all Bokharians: their not being able to do so has given cause to the Persians, their hereditary foes, to indulge insulting sayings at their expense, such as the following:—" He is as stupid as a Bokharian," "a Bokharian stupidity" (Nemaketi-bokari) (hikmatibokari?). They use also the following expression when they want to cry down any pieces of poetry, *viz.*, "Shehir bukari" (Bokharian poetry), or "Shahri, Shah Tahmati" (because Shah Thames II. had made some very bad verses).

The trading route from Semipalatinsk to Cashmere.

From Semi-Fubat * to Ileh, a month's march, during which hordes of Kossacks † are often met with. In the neighbourhood of Semi-Fubat flows a river; two others flow near Ileh: the space between Semi-Fubat and Ileh is intersected by mountains and plains.

From Ileh to Aksoo the distance is about sixteen "Eurtunys."‡ Ten rivers are crossed. Aksoo is smaller than Ileh. From Aksoo to Yarkand we calculate sixteen Eurtunys. To reach this town, which is very big, and which has Customs Officers, a mountain chain, very high and completely covered with snow and ice, must be crossed. One remains in Yarkand a few days to take in provisions and to make other preparations for the journey: this done, the march towards Thibet § is commenced. After five days' march, the Eurtuny ‖ of Khataij is reached: from hence the road continues between two rows of high mountains. The rocky ground is sometimes intersected by mountain streams. Seventy-two such are crossed before coming to a high mountain called the "Kara-curen-padishah," which stands in the middle of the road. In former days a town existed here;

---

* Semipalatinsk is generally called by the Orientals Semi-Fubat.

† Properly Kirghizzees, for only the middle and lesser hordes are called Kossacks; the seventeen tribes of the larger horde only call themselves Kirghizzees.

‡ The Eurtuny contains about 25 to 30 Versts.

§ This seems to be the correct way of pronouncing it, though the Orientals sometimes write it Tubbet.

‖ Eurtuny here means a geographical measurement something like the Ly of the Chinese.

further on, the exhalations from the ground cause man and horse to be covered with boils and sores and makes the atmosphere unwholesome. After this, one reaches another chain, whose perpetual snow the sun cannot thaw.*   Upon this a stream is met with that is crossed fifteen times.

For the next four stations there exist no water, no wood, and no pasturage for the horses. Accordingly, for the seven days required to pass this country, one has to distribute one camel-load amongst two, and use another horse to carry the forage, as well as a second to carry food for every two men. Then for another fifty † days' march one passes through a country in which there are no signs of cultivation, the ground being nothing but rock.

Approaching Thibet a mountain is crossed; there are two stages during which the yak and dogs ‡ are the only animals in use. Thibet is a town situated on the rise of a mountain; the Governor's Palace crowns the summit: the houses of the inhabitants are situated all round on the slopes, and only cease at the foot of the hill. The appearance of the inhabitants is saddening. They are clothed from head to foot in black. Their food consists of nothing but tea and milk, and of a kind of soup, and dumplings made of barley. The merchants have to report themselves to the Governor to have their merchandize taxed ; at this visit every one of them presents him with a tea cup and some tea. They drink tea with His Excellency, and then return to their homes. They wait a few days until the Governor has examined and taxed their merchandize, then they depart from Thibet, and, for twenty days, march along the edge of a mountain in the bed of a big river before arriving at Ischardjaï. The Raja of this place levies a duty, salaams to the merchants, and makes them a few presents. A finer country commences here (a Customs Officer shows himself a day's march out of Cashmere §). If, on account of the large quantity of merchandize, he cannot, during the day, value them all, he seals the bales with his own seal, and finishes his work after they have entered the town. A caravan going from Semi-Fubat to Thibet has to collect fresh provisions in each town through which it passes, in this case seven times.

It does not seem out of place here to add a few notes regarding what has occurred in the Khanate of Cashmere and Affghanistan between the years 1811 and 1817, taken from the above-mentioned memoirs of Mechi-Raphael, thus adding to the history of these countries, as related to us by Elphinstone :—

" Fatih Khan, the Sirdar Mahmood of the Khan of Cabul, an enter-prising, ferocious, and ambitious man, long since exercised full power over the mind and person of his Sovereign, whom he kept in a sort of captivity, fully dependent on his own wishes. Squandering the riches of

---

* This is the very spot now-a-days called the Karah-ghoni Tagh (i.e., the dark mountain).

† Accordingly, the journey from Semipalatinsk to Thibet would take 124 days' marching: this exceeds by 28 days the time given by Mechi-Raphael, a Jew from Cabul, whose memoir I have before me, and who has done this journey several times. It certainly seems impossible accurately to give the time required, as travelling in moun-tainous countries intersected with rivers is very much dependent on circumstances, also, more or less, on the amount of rain-fall.

‡ A kind of ox peculiar for its large and curly tail.

§ The town of Cashmere, according to Mechi-Raphael, is twenty marches from Delhi.

his royal master, as well those squeezed out of the inhabitants, he made the Affghans of Cabul and Candahar his friends, and at the head of a devoted army, he attacked and took possession of all the neighbouring States. At last he also wished to possess Cashmere; his first attack on this kingdom proved unsuccessful, for the forts of Peshawur and Attock made a good resistance and blocked his way.

"Fatih Khan, despairing ever to take the country from this side, began privately to negotiate with Runjeet Sing, the Ruler of the Punjab, and proposed jointly to attack and take Cashmere, dividing the spoils of the Khan's Treasury and land: consequently, Fatih Khan, at the head of an army, entered Hindostan, and, joining Runjeet Sing's troops, attacked Cashmere from a side the least expected. Ata Mahomed Khan was obliged to shut himself up in the town of Cashmere, where Fatih Khan besieged him, and at last necessity compelled him to capitulate. The conditions were that Ata Mahomed Khan should give up to the conqueror all his treasures, which consisted chiefly in jewelry and precious stones, and in return should be allowed to leave the country unmolested, taking with him all his family and all those who chose to follow him into exile. The dethroned monarch fled to Zadi-Kamran, the son of Shah Mahmood, and Governor of Candahar; he also succeeded in deceiving his oppressor by handing over to him, as his treasure, a quantity of false stones instead of the real ones, estimated at eighty million rupees, and which he luckily managed to take away with him. On arrival at Candahar the Khan employed his treasure in securing adherents and the means of regaining his throne, whilst Fatih Khan was busy completing the conquest of Cashmere. Meanwhile, the Governor of Attock and Peshawur, hearing the fate of their master, gave up their posts to Runjeet Sing for certain sums of money.

"Hardly was Fatih Khan in possession of the whole territory than he began to think how he could get rid of his ally. On some frivolous pretext he sent all his Indian troops back to their country, then openly declared his intention of not dividing the country, &c., they had conquered with Runjeet Sing. But he did not long enjoy the fruits of his treachery, for the son of Shah Mahmood had, by means of the Khan of Cashmere's wealth, gathered a considerable army, with which he suddenly appeared in Cabul, and, having beaten Fatih Khan's troops, replaced his father on the throne and took the traitor prisoner. According to the last accounts (1817), it seems that Fatih Khan has paid with his life for the crime by which he had earned the hatred of all the inhabitants of these regions."

APPENDIX II.

About Tartary in an ethnographical point of view.

The Asiatic people, who in Russia are known as Tartars, have a rather flat nose, high cheek bones, little beards, with small and sometimes squinting eyes. Tschingis Khan, with the aid of his Moguls, conquered the Tartars, who were completely embodied in his army. As they formed the larger number, the conquerors adopted their language, barbarous as it was. From this mixture of the Tartar and Mogul race spring all the people at present living in Turkistan.

Indeed, there is a very great difference between the features of a Kirghizzee Uzbek, Turcoman, Aneymak, and those of a Turkish Osmanli, a Tartar of Kasan, or of the Crimea. Still modern geographers declare that the Kirghizzees have pure Tartar features, very similar to those of Europeans; but such a statement is unfounded, and it is impossible to mistake Kirghizzees and the other Mogul Tartars for Kalmuks, for they are unlike in build and have not such marked and pronounced features.

The flight of the Kalmuk Torguts from the steppes of the Volga in 1770 through the Kirghiz deserts, where many of these fugitives have been left behind, has no doubt also led to the Kalmuk physiognomy being much varied, some proofs of which are still found amongst the Kirghizzees. With them it is considered a disgrace to be called a "Kalmuk," for the Torguts had fallen into slavery in this land.

The dimensions given to Tartary in an ethnographical sense are in my opinion not large enough, for at present only the Tartars of Siberia, of Kasan, of Astrakhan, of the Crimea, and of the countries lying towards Caspian Sea, are considered as belonging to that race; whereas all Turkish Osmanlis belong to it. The Tartars that have remained, and are predominant in the country which is by us designated as Little Bokhara (a name unknown in Asia, instead of which Chinese Tartary would be more appropriate), have certainly been conquered by the Kalmuks, but have not been extirpated. The Tartar language is still generally spoken in Kashgar, Yarkand, Khoten, and Aksoo, so that these countries in an ethnographical point of view belong to Tartary. I can in no way agree with those who think that Tartary, in a geographical point of view, is bordered to the east by the Beloor, and to the south-east by the Hindoo Kush. According to this idea, one would include races of men who are in every respect not Tartars, and leave out Chinese Turkistan, which, in reality, is inhabited by none but Tartars.

It seems to me, therefore, to be more to the purpose if we substitute the more geographically correct denomination of Tartary for the one now in vogue. I include in it the whole tract of land between the Irtisch, the Attai, the Sarbagtai, the Mussart or Mutagh, the Beloor, the Hindoo Kush, the Mountain Ghaour, which stretches along the north of Persia, the east coast of the Caspian Sea, the Ural Mountain chain, and the northern boundary of the Kirghiz steppe.

The so-called "Independent Tartary," which is inhabited by free Tartars, is more suitably designated Independent Mogul Tartary, and the vast country inhabited by the Moguls, "Mongolia."

APPENDIX III.

The Khanates of Khiva, Khokhan, and Kashgar.

Regarding the Khanate of Khiva I shall say but little, as Colonel Mourariew has published his journey to that land, to which book I refer anybody wishing for further details.

A daughter of Albufaiz, Khan of Bokhara, and a contemporary of Nadir Shah, married a Khan of Khiva, named Kaip, who was born a Kirghizzee. Mahomed Rahim, the present Khan of Khiva, is a descendant of his; he is a man as much favoured as enterprising, and who has succeeded in subjecting several Turcoman hordes in the south-east and west. His territory extends from the Caspian Sea to the frontier of Bokhara. To the south of Khezarist or Hezarasp, the most southern Khivan town, as well as to the west to about the 40th degree of latitude, the Turcoman hordes dwell who recognize the Khan of Khiva as the supreme power, and who are at enmity with the hordes living on the northern frontier of Khorassan and Daghestan, and belong to those who rebuilt the town Seragh, situated about two hundred versts from Mawri. The Khan of Khiva, after having taken Mawri and Seragh from them, gave it back to them to keep in order to protect this part of his territory from Persian invasion.

The Turcomans who inhabit the eastern shores of the Caspian Sea are in communication with Russia, and derive all their flour from thence. As they are nearly without exception deadliest enemies of the Persians, they sent an embassy to General Ritcher in 1813 to beg him not to make a separate Treaty with the Persians, as they would, so they said, "gain decisive victories over the common enemy."

The avaricious Mahomed Rahim appears to be pleased when he hears of the plundering of Russian and Bokharian caravans, and the Khivans often make raids into the heart of the Bokharian country, although they dare not take the field openly, for Bokhara contains six times the population of Khiva.

In 1808 the Khan of Bokhara conquered Khiva, but gave it back to its Ruler, Valedi Nassir, the brother of the present Khan. The latter often attacks the Kirghizzees, and has made many of them prisoners; he forces them to settle down in and cultivate his territory, aiding them with irrigation canals: he has only just completed one leading from the Amoo, a hundred and twenty versts in length.

Of all the towns in the Khanate of Khiva, New-Oorg is the most important with regard to commerce; it is the spot where all caravans meet, but still it does not contain a caravanserai for the depositing of merchandize.

The inhabitants of Khiva are partly Uzbeks, the conquerors of the land, and partly Turcomans: the nomads are originally Kara-Kalpaks, Arabese, Kirghiz, a few Jews, and partly Sartyrs, or Tadjiks, of whom we have already spoken.

Although the Bokharians and Khivans are of the same origin and profess the same religion, still, as regards culture and civilization, the former have always been more advanced than the latter. The Khivan Colleges have never attained the same reputation as those of Bokhara, and altogether they are in a lower scale of civilization, as is seen in their being less attentive to agriculture, in their poorer dwellings, restricted commerce, little wealth, and in their rougher manners and customs.

The climate is here a little colder, but the nature of the soil is in both countries pretty much the same; they have the same productions, although the harvests in Bokhara are perhaps a little more plentiful: silk in particular is more scarce in Khiva than in Bokhara, and bread is much dearer there too.

The Khanate of Khokhan lies to the east and north-east of Bokhara; since the annexation of Tashkend in 1805, and of Chinese Turkistan and its dependencies in 1815, it has much increased.

Its boundaries are to the west, the Sir Daria; to the south, Kashghai-diwani; to the east, Alatagh; and to the north, Kazaklu-djulak and Soosac. Its most southern frontier towns are Ochand and Takht Suleiman. The territory of Ak-Masjid on the Sir, through which all caravans coming and going from Bokhara to Petropolovsk must pass, is well known under that name, given it through the fact of a mosque having once upon a time stood here, of which at present nothing remains but a ruin. I am told that the tribe Jhun of the larger horde generally roams about in these regions.

A hundred versts to the east of Ak-Masjid is Karaklu-djulak, a small town of the Sir; from here one can see in the distance the northern peaks of the Alatagh, which chain, taking a direction away from the Sir, loses itself gradually in the steppes.

Soosai is a small mountain fort. Up till 1798 Turkistan was under the yoke of Kirghiz Sultans. Taghai, the last of them, was dethroned by the Juns-koja, the Khan of Tashkend, and fled to Bokhara. Turkistan contains a fort surrounded by a ditch two and a half toises in width, which, in case of danger from the enemy, can be filled with water. The town consists of about two thousand mud huts and twenty-two wells; the Karachic flows within five versts, and is used for irrigation. The inhabitants of Turkistan are Kirghizzees, and a small number of Uzbeks. Of all the saints here interred, Kara-Ahmed Koja is the most honored; in the vicinity of the mosque bearing his name is an enormous cauldron, at least two toises in diameter; it rests on a pedestal of solid iron, and is used for cooking food for the poor, which is given by the rich on certain holy days.

Tashkend, which contains at least three thousand mud houses, is surrounded by a mud wall, now in ruins; the houses are also in a more ruinous condition, much worse than those in Bokhara. Khiva contains ten colleges, three of which are built on the same plan as those of Bokhara. Small canals leading from the Cherchic, which flows about twenty versts to the south of Tashkend, supply the town with water.

The country of Tashkend produces cotton and silk. The Beg's artillery consists of small pieces, carried, as in Persia, on camels' backs. In the neighbourhood are the villages of Jiti-Reerd, Seyram, Kara-bura,

Tshungha, Eeun, and a few more; they are inhabited by Usbeks, and only a small number of Tadjiks and Turkistans are seen in them; Jews never.

Moreover, I have made many enquiries concerning the different routes, especially as regards the exact distances of the towns of Turkistan, Tashkend, Khokhan, Khojend, Ura-tepah, Samarcand, and Bokhara, and am convinced as to their situation being wrongly indicated in the large Russian Map of Central Asia. Regarding the Kirghizzee Steppe it is more accurate than the one by Mr. Arrowsmith, but as regards the length of Samarcand, the course of the Sir between Khokhan and Turkistan, the situation of Khokhan, &c., &c., it is not to be compared to that of Mr. Arrowsmith, and this is the reason why, in making my map, I had more reliance on the latter map, although I have, in many instances, deviated from it also.

Khojend is situated on the banks of the Sir. This town is passed when journeying from Ura-tepah to Khokhan; in doing this one makes a large detour, which enables one to avoid a mountainous country not always passable. One could, I dare say, travel direct from Marghalan to Samarcand if the Tshenga Kirghizzees did not always plunder the traveller. Khojend is a fort, and, like Bokhara, surrounded by fields and gardens.

Khokhan, situated about ten versts from the Sir, contains at least sixteen thousand houses, and is nearly as large as Bokhara: the town is supplied with water by canals leading from the Sir. The town is not protected by a wall, but the castle is so; it is made of mud with two gateways of brick.

Khokhan contains four caravanserais, continually filled with foreign merchants; it is the central market-place between Tashkend, Kashgar, and Bokhara. The Khanate of Khokhan has the very same products as Bokhara, but it is smaller and less powerful. The countries are at enmity with one another, and often go to war. Ten years ago the Bokharians took possession of Ura-tepah, which was formerly an independent district.

Omar, the present Khan of Khokhan, and son of his predecessor Narbuta, is universally respected and honored. He lives at peace with Khiva, being related to the Khan of that place, as also to the Khan of Badakschan, whose daughter he has married.

Marghalan, it is said, is as large as Khokhan: it is an ancient town; so are Andijan and Namanghan.

Och is situated at the foot of the Takt Suleiman, a mountain chain, whose name means "Solomon's throne;" it is of small importance, but much wealth is brought to it by pilgrims: the place of pilgrimage is a small square house, built on a lower range of the chain. According to popular tradition, Solomon is said to have killed a camel on this spot, and the blood-stains are still to be seen in the rock. Any one suffering from rheumatism, or any such illness, has only to lay himself on a certain flat stone, and he is immediately cured. Mr. Nasarow declares that he saw the ruins of two large buildings, under which he found a cave. Superstition brings a crowd of people to Och every year.

Between Och and Kashgar there are no towns or cultivation; the country is mountainous; the so-called black or wild Kirghizzees roam about in the Ala tagh with their hordes. These hordes have their eyes close to one another, and a more squinting appearance than other Kirghizzees; and altogether their physiognomies are more like those of the Kalmucks. They are brave, and their horses are as fleet and hardy as those of the Circassians. A few Chinese merchants, who unite in small caravans, trade with these Kirghizzees in the Ala tagh. They come across from Kashgar and Koulja, and have never anything to fear from these savages.

The Kirghizzees spend the winter months in the valleys, leaving them in the summer; they grow barley and millet. Their favourite abode is in the Jedi-soo, or the "country of the seven rivers."

In the spring of 1818 they plundered a few villages in the neighbourhood of Tashkend, but this raid was severely revenged by five thousand Khokhans, who made a successful expedition against them in their own haunts. I have gathered all this information from a Tartar who had been taken prisoner by these nomads, and had spent seven years amongst them; he assured me that some of the peaks of the Alatagh were covered with perpetual snow, and that birch trees and firs were often to be seen. This same Tartar was once exchanged for thirteen horses; on another occasion he formed part of a bride's dowry. He at last managed to escape with the help of some Chinese merchants; he remained some time in Kashgar, and then came to Bokhara, from whence we took him with us back to Russia.

Between Kashgar and Och this Tartar had to cross several rivers, and passed through a very mountainous country, the mountains of which were covered with snow and the climate very cold. Another traveller assured me that the climate of Telik was nothing but a continuous winter, and that, on account of the snow in the valleys, it was hardly possible even to choose one of three roads for trading purposes.

According to all information I could gather on the subject, the Bokharians call Chinese Turkistan, Alti-Chakan, or the land of six cities: these are Kasbgar, Yarkand, Khoten, Aksoo, and the two Ilys.

Kashgar is a large town garrisoned by Chinamen, and it is easily accessible. It is situated on the Kashgar, a river which flows into the Kijitsoo (red water), which flows between Kashgar and Yarkand.

To get to Cashmere from Kashgar, one has to pass through Yarkand, where the Tartar language is still spoken, and through the towns of Large and Small Thibet. On account of the country being mountainous, the caravans make but short daily marches; moreover, it is impossible to use any animals but horses.

Yarkand is four marches distant from Kashgar, and is, according to the description of Raphael Danibeg, a Georgian Nobleman, prettily situated in the centre of a patch of underwood. It has a garrison of at least 2,000 Chinamen. The Commander is called Aniban. The town contains about three thousand Chinese merchants.

The climate, on the whole, is good; the water bad: there are no fine buildings, but the inhabitants are in easy circumstances. Moreover, the autumn is here most unhealthy, more so than in many other similar places: at this time of the year a curious sort of dust comes down like rain and creates great uneasiness. The dampness of the atmosphere often generates a kind of small red insect called by the inhabitants

" Karbite," whose sting is nearly always fatal.   When the inhabitants see
this dust fall instead of rain, they anticipate good crops, and bad ones
if it only rains.   This dust is so dense, that the sun's rays cannot pene-
trate it : at the same time it is so fine that it enters through the slightest
opening ; it generally lasts seven or eight days.

Great Thibet is distant thirty to forty marchs from Kashgar and Yar-
kand.   About twenty-two marches from the former, half way, is Small
Thibet.   It seems to me to be very probable that the towns here called
Great and Small Thibet are most likely those known by the name of
Ladak and Draouse or Dervazeh, but it is remarkable that no Tartar
knows these towns by the latter names, but only as Great and Small
Thibet, as also did Russian merchants who travelled from Semipalatinsk
to Cashmere.

According to my calculations, Great Thibet is situated in 35° 50′ N.
Lat. and 76° 35′ E. Long. of Paris, and, according to the above-mentioned Georgian, it is built on hillocks surrounded by high mountains,
which only produce a few oats.   The inhabitants pour milk into the oat
flour, and then bake it with butter : they are so poor that this is their
only nourishment.   It is here the custom that in a house containing
several brothers one single woman becomes the wife of all of them ; the
children are named after the eldest brother, whom alone they look upon
as their father.

Between Kashgar and Cashmere there are no other towns than those
just mentioned, in the vicinity of which may be found a village or two.
Great and Small Thibet are surrounded by gardens, and the houses are
said to be similar to those in Russia, of wood with very high roofs.
The inhabitants worship the Lama and are idolators.

From Kashgar to Semipalatinsk is one hundred and fifty-five
marches, twelve of which are to Aksoo, and five and twenty to Koulja
or Ily.   It says in the excellent work of Mr. Ritter that the most
comfortable route lies through the mountains north of Kashgar.

Close to Aksoo I have heard of this statement being confirmed ;
nevertheless, the caravans have good reasons for taking a more circuitous
route.

For the whole distance between Koulja and Aksoo, they keep as
close as possible to the Chinese frontier, feeling certain of not being
plundered ; just as the Khivan caravans, wanting to reach Orenburg,
go via Saratchik or Saratchikova, keeping close to the Ural Mountains,
instead of taking the shorter route from Khiva to Orenburg right
through the Kirghizzee Steppes.

The most important stream between Koulja and Semipalatinsk is
the Alaghaz, which flows to the north of the Tarbaghalaij.   The highest
mountains here are the Tschowlk-Karaghay, the crossing of which takes
four days.

There are two Kouljas, the great and the little one ; both are on the
bank of the Ily, by which name they are also designated, and are forty
versts apart from one another.   Little Koulja is a fort, which is quite
unlike any Bokharian fort ; it is very similar to a European one, having
salient angles and regular bastions.   The gates are closed every evening
at sunset, when a gun is fired.   Great Koulja, which lies to the south of
the former and in a Chinese Djomgarry, contains about ten thousand

" Tshapans" or Chinese infantry. This town has six gates and nearly nine thousand houses of mud, wood, and some even of stone; all of them have roofs as in Russia. Koulja is not surrounded by cultivated land, but thirty versts off there are a few dozen Chinese villages. Besides the Djomgarry Tartars, there are Chinese to be found in Koulja, who form the greater part of the inhabitants, and who are distinguished from the Kara-Kilaizes or black Chinamen, whose wives' feet are of celebrated smallness.

The Ily at Koulja is only about a hundred feet wide, and is fordable in the summer time.

APPENDIX IV.

The Khanates of Hissar, Kulal, Ranird, Badakschan, and Chersabes.

To the south of Khokhan and to the west of Bokhara there are several Khanates and independent people, who are partly Mahomedans, and partly not; they are looked upon as infidels by the Moslems. All these people inhabit mountainous countries.

The wealthiest of these Khanates is that of Hissar, whose Khan resides in the town of the same name, which is situated about fifteen versts to the west of the banks of the Saridjour or Kafir-inhan. He is the father-in-law of Khan Atalik, and a faithful ally of the Khan of Bokhara.

The town of Hissar contains about three thousand houses, and is situated in a well-cultivated and fertile valley. The inhabitants are nearly all Uzbeks. One meets only a few Tadjiks; these are mostly wealthy. It is related that the Uzbeks sometimes bring millet into the market-place for sale, and when they find they cannot get rid of it all they invariably throw it away, so as to save themselves the trouble of carrying it back. They possess large herds of cattle, and altogether are pretty well off.

The towns belonging to the Khanate of Hissar are Deinaon, the next in size to Hissar, Saridjour, Tupalak, Regai, or Regara, Karatagh, Deehtabad, Tshok Mazar, and Khojatamon, in which place a Moslem saint lies buried.

Ramid, about a hundred versts to the north of Hissar, is rather an important town. Its Khan is able to put ten thousand men in the field. In the vicinity of Ramid we find the highest mountain of the country.

Kulal, a town of about three thousand houses, lies to the east of Hissar, on the road from Badakschan to Khokhan, and is independent. All the towns are inhabited by Uzbeks, a great number of whom are agriculturalists.

To the south of all these towns we find the Khanate of Badakschan; its capital is of the same name, but is also sometimes known as Fayzabad: it is situated on the banks of the Badakschan, a tributary of the Amoo. This is one of the most important Khanates in these regions, and yet its chief staple consists only of Lapis-lazuli, and it is, besides, not on the high road used by caravans.

To get to Cashmere from Badakschan, one generally travels *via* Kashgar or Peshawur: this is in consequence of the mountains between Badakschan and Cashmere being impassable.

In the mountainous tract to the east of Bokhara and north of Hissar dwell the Ghalishas, a poor but independent population, who profess the Seminite Islam religion.

Russian travellers have given them the name of Oriental Persians: they speak Persian, and know no other language; their physiognomy differ very much from that of the Tadjiks; their complexion is brown, and even darker than that of the Bokharian Arabs. They live in miserable huts, at the foot of hills; are all agricultural, and possess a few oxen and very few horses.

Matcha and Jognaon are towns inhabited by these Ghaltshas; they are situated to the north of Khokhan. Further to the east, the country becomes more and more mountainous and unknown. One hears of there being a people there called Kaffirs, who are very wild. After leaving Karatighan, one finds no more Mahomedans: the inhabitants of that town are, by no means, cruel. The dreaded Kaffirs dwell in Kalei-khonur, a town also called Derwazeh, and situated on the banks of a river of the same name.

The country about here is so steep and rocky that one is often obliged to get off one's horse, and to lead him by the bridle.

The Derwazeh contains in its bed a little gold ore, and this induces the avarice of the Bokharians from time to time to hazard their lives in order to get some of the precious metal. For this purpose they throw into the river leather bags fastened to ropes; these soon fill up with mud, sand, and sometimes gold, which can then be easily separated, but it is never found pure: in its alloyed state it is as 18 to 21 to its pure state. This method seems to explain a passage in Herodotus, in which he speaks of Indians bringing gold to the surface in this same manner.

To the south and the east of Badakschan dwell the Siknan or Siah-pouch, a half-wild, half-nomad race, who ignore Mahomedanism. Their appellation means "black clothes," and is given them on account of their dress, which consists merely of black sheep skins. The shortest road from Khokban to Peshawur leads through their territory, and through Tschitral, their capital, but the country is so rocky that it is seldom passable.

The Khan of Badakschan is often at war with this tribe, and the prisoners made are sold in Bokhara by Badakschan merchants.

In the centre of Bokhara there exists an independent Khanate, viz., that of Chersabes or Shehri-sabz. This last name is derived from the capital, which is situated on the banks of a river of the same name. This river is also called Kachka, and flows by Karchi, an important Bokharian town.

The Khanate Chersabes (Shahr-sabz?) owes its independence to this river on more than one occasion, as by it the inhabitants can inundate all the surrounding country, which in itself is quite enough to protect it from Bokharian invasion. Besides, the Uzbeks of Chersabes are renowned for their bravery.

This Khanate was annexed to Bokhara in the reign of Mahomed Rahim Khan, but was enabled to regain its independence at his death in 1751. The loss of this country must have been felt very much by the Bokharians, especially as all the ground on both sides of the stream which runs through it is very fertile and covered with wood used for dyeing, and with cotton, which products are exchanged for Russian iron and leather merchandize.

The Khan of Chersabes is able at a push to put about 20,000 men in the field; the towns under his rule are Kilab and Donab (two forts), Pitabaneh, Jakabak, Uta-kurghan. Moreover, Chersabes is remarkable for one more reason, viz., it is built on the same spot where in former days stood the village Kech, the birth-place of "the renowned Timoor."

www.ingramcontent.com/pod-product-compliance
Lightning Source LLC
Chambersburg PA
CBHW081520040426
42447CB00013B/3281